I0720261

Reckoning: A Chorus, Divergent
Electronic Edition: Fall 2025

Editor: C.G. Aubrey

Reckoning *is a communal effort.*
Editorial staff, in alphabetical order:

C.G. Aubrey
E.C. Barrett
Octavia Cade
Priya Chand
Michael J. DeLuca
Tim Fab-Eme
Joseph Hope
Ruth Joffre
Aaron Kling
Andrew Kozma
Ellis Nye
Jackie Roberti
Catherine Rockwood
Bernie Jean Schiebeling

Cover and text ornament by Abi Stevens
Cover design by Priya Chand

Reckoning Press
206 East Flint Street
Lake Orion, MI 48362
www.reckoning.press
distributed by IngramSpark
 ISSN 2474-7327
e-ISBN 978-1-955360-17-3
print ISBN 978-1-955360-16-6

Reckoning:
A Chorus, Divergent

Contents

Editorial

C. G. Aubrey

In the US this year, we neurodivergent folks have heard a lot about what we cannot do or will never do. Our differences have been increasingly pathologized, demonized, and used to deny us basic respect and decency. Our diagnoses have been dismissed, our personal autonomy, access to medications, and medical care threatened. All because we will never write a poem? That is true for some of us, but poetry is hardly a standard skill set among neurotypicals. It is, after all, uncommon experiences and mindsets that shape creativity. What is poetry, after all, but the manifestation of uncommon wonder?

I began this editorial back in May, when we here at Reckoning first decided to produce this special reprint collection. This was seven drafts ago. Each time I sat down to write, I found myself wanting to avoid vulnerability and to explain . . . well, everything. I wanted to be certain we all understood that neurodivergence is more than ADHD and Autism Spectrum Disorder; that the face of neurodivergence is neither white nor male nor USAmerican. Neurodivergence is complex and intersectional, and what is considered neurodivergent can vary greatly with cultural norms. I wanted to define terms and provide helpful links. I was drafting a rebuttal to a certain US public official's list, both scholarly and emotional. Then I realized that I was coming perilously close to defending our existence.

We should not need this kind of defence (though too often we do). We do, however, need acknowledgement, and we deserve celebration. Neurodivergent folks live with differences and difficulties that shouldn't be dismissed, but likewise, with determination and daring that cannot be disregarded. We are out here, every day, doing the deep, meaningful work of living. And there is much work to do. There are voices to find, voices to lift, especially among the most vulnerable of us. There is art to create. There are discoveries to be made, policies to change, and stereotypes to dismantle. We'll get to all of those, and more, because

We *have been doing, all along, the very things* we continue to be told we can't.

If we must speak in generalities (because this is apparently what we do, /irato/), let us speak instead of neurodivergent curiosity and creativity, of the many artists, writers, and, yes, poets among us. Let us speak our devotion to making sense of life's chaos, and not ignore the ongoing contributions of neurodivergent scientists and scholars. Let us speak of our strong sensitivity to injustice, of the many neurodivergent individuals who pursue careers in social work and activism. We should also speak of our determination to connect with others, to understand and to be understood. There are communication deficits among many of us (this is also a cultural malady affecting neurotypicals, but never mind that), and yet we persist. We listen for words unspoken; we acknowledge the silenced. We continue, despite so many obstacles, to find our voices, to speak for ourselves and for those who cannot.

Among the works collected from *Reckoning*'s first decade, you'll find these refrains. Short stories like T.K. Rex's "SQUAWKER AND DOLPHIN SWIMMING TOGETHER" and Taylor Jones's "Possession" build communication bridges between disparate communities and species. Powerful works like Mari Ness's poem "Green Leaves Against the Wind" and Ariadne Starling's essay "The X That Means Both Death and Hope" remind us that justice is both personal and political, inextricably intertwined. Jacob Coffin beautifully imagines a greener, more tenable, infinitely possible future, repurposed from an unsustainable present. We meet our current uncertainties with actionable hope.

This special neurodivergent reprint collection is for us—to celebrate, to encourage, and to fortify our neurodivergent contributors, readers, and supporters. However, it is shared in hope and gratitude with everyone, wherever you might fit within humanity's sprawling neurodiversity. If you have found yourself a little lost in reading this editorial, please know that I did, in fact, find a way to over-explain. In the back pages of this issue you'll find definitions, explanations, and resources.

When I consider the struggles of this present moment, and the voices that seek to drown out those of neurodivergent individuals and communities, I am reminded of nature's song. Cacophony seems an overused word, and yet it is filled with breath, with the rise and fall of syllables, notes dulcet and discordant. It embraces every cadence of birdcall, every splash and screech, scurry and slither; it holds within it the dissonance of the chase, the flee, the sweet stench of decay, the quiet flights, and the screaming iridescence. There is room for the consonance and dissonance of humanity's harmony, though many of us would rather not consider ourselves a part of it, and some of us try too hard to decide who gets to sing at all. We forget that the chorus has always been divergent, that the moth's silence is not unspeaking.

There is poetry in its wings.

C.G. Aubrey is a queer, AuDHD writer and outdoor enthusiast obsessed with yellow leaves, swamp rainbows, and em dashes. She holds dual-masters degrees in US History and Religious Studies and often finds inspiration at the intersection of cultural memory, religion, and the environment. Her story "A Predatory Transience" appeared in Reckoning in 2023; she's been editing here ever since. Find her occasionally on Bluesky @cgaubrey.bsky.social, Instagram @c.g.aubrey, and www.cgaubrey.com.

The World Ended in Ice

Adam Stemple

The world ended in ice
as scientists predicted
lab coat Noahs
ignored
as they counted the animals
two by two
into their ark
and lifted off

We who are left
shiver
in the cold
in the dark
in our ignorance and greed
forgotten sinners
with no dove
to fly from Ararat

Adam Stemple (www.adamstemple.com) is an author, poet, musician, web designer, artist, and professional card player.

After Erysichthon

Kaye Boesme

The whole world is a feast of runaway craving,
of a curse that has outrun its uses.
Early on, our ancestors twisted up,
moved root through rock, spread fragile first leaves wide.
All land was new, mountainous, unsoiled.

The forests that grew have lasted so long,
spreading across the world at glacial pace.
We stretch and recede, grow up and move out.
Famine and war will parch your lips, drag you
below the Earth where we feast on your flesh.

What is breath but the ambrosia of trees?
You suckle our gaseous exhalations.
We wean you down to Hades at your death.

Who are these children who warm,
strain, and devour the wide earth,
cornucopia fraying,
desert bursting at its seams?

We are the trees who were once never wronged,
not axe-culled, not forced to grow through fences.
The Thunderer and those bright kin alone
touched us, burned us, but we claimed the wide land.
Forgotten myths say we gave birth to you.

We danced with Hermes on sloping mountains,
later with Pan whom my tall sister bore.
To me came Artemis' strict retinue.
We ran in those places no man dared see.
Then your people grew up and tamed the wilds.

The gifts we brought you at your birth were myrrh,
frankincense, and storax, life-giving scents
beloved of gods, the sweat from our bark.

Erysichthon was condemned
as he felled that first grove.
Its nymph guardian begged, and
sap pooled at her feet like blood.

Forests fell back, expanding horizons.
When we seduced you, we brought you to groves,
breathed in the incense and breath you exhaled,
taught you secrets of bees and bitter plants.
You worshipped us alongside stone statues.

We know which of you swung the axe to cut
deep into the sap-giving arteries,
your grandmothers and sisters cut to stumps.
This is how we learned how to give curses.
Now all-consuming hunger binds us all.

Persephone opens wide arms to those
initiated into mysteries
shining like white cypress bark and gold leaves.

We punish with a hunger.
That murderer devoured
until he bit down deep on
his own tender flesh, ripped hard.

Our lives stretch so long that none can compare.
Curses work best when exercised lightly.
Torchers of nymphs, bearers of distress, you
smashed so many of us, pried open trunks,
carved once-sacred wood to ford the wide sea.

Rage boils thick in our sap when nymphs die.
We witness trunks uprooted, roots twisted
hard from a fall driven by gravity.
More often, they're intact, dead from disease.
Dryads decay hidden in scrapped branches.

What you give the forest opens the way.
Here in mountain places, philosophers
found pathways in sunbeams mottled with green.

The hexed consume without end,
now without limit or death.
Their tools extract Plouton's wealth;
all the world weeps out poison.

In perfumed shrines where our secret teachings
saturated air, ground, and cool water,
offerings blackened cave ceilings with soot.
We cannot suckle those who have breath, not
until your hearts root down in awe of place.

Make white cakes covered in sticky honey.
Go to the chamber of the ones who dwell
among the countless wronged dead, they who howl,
who listen to sapless whispers of shades.
Pacify them and be made whole again.

Come to the mountain, come to the gorge-nook.
The water we pull up through our roots tastes
sweet of nectar and metal, wilds and waste.

We repeat the dead ones' names.
This world is old, the list great,
our curses worn like old silt.

We watch all in reflections
metal and glass leave, your eyes
searching, tamed lightning your guide.

You linger in pallid storefront lights, dark
patterns ghosting across your distracted
faces, forest yet close. Look up. See us.

Sooner or later, your meandering
steps will remember sacred rites once more.
Sooner or later, emptiness will tire
you—you will reach for the wholeness of yore.

Kaye Boesme is a poet, conlanger, and writer. Her poetry has appeared in *Kaleidotrope*, *Illumen*, and *Eternal Haunted Summer*, and she has a short story out in *The Society of Misfit Stories Presents*. More information about her work is available at kayeboesme.com, or on her Substack at pangrammatike.substack.com. Boesme has a background in library and information science, so while she did not set out to know strange things, strangeness happened upon her.

Before Times Shells & Gifts

L. McKnight

Dustin picks up the sand dollar and rubs it between his fingers, feels the strange chalkiness of it. He studies the delicate etchings, the five-pointed flower, before putting it in his mouth and closing his eyes. The texture against his tongue. The light salt.

Organics are some of the coolest things left over from the Before Times, and Dustin feels like finding one must be a good omen. He knows some of the marsh people collect them, stash them in the little mud jars they use to store treasures, alongside the metal circles once used for trade.

This particular organic, a sand dollar, is exceedingly rare, especially for this particular stretch of the Nouveau Gulf Coast. Dustin knows this because he is a collector, or a trader rather, owner and operator of Before Times Shells & Gifts, Hand-Harvested Souvenirs from Pre-Armageddon Louisiana. He drives a bulky Before Times van, from BT 1900 and 84 to be exact, filled with artifacts carefully selected from the seaside: scraps of metal from barges and oil rigs, wooden bits of shrimp boats, the occasional *tou-lou-lou* shell or tide-beaten fiddle string, or maybe a flashy Carnival doubloon.

As he moves down the shore, past the raggedy old pier, his heart picks up pace, knowing the sand dollar is of high value—and not just to the petro-tourists who pay billions of solar-credits to visit the rigs. The sand dollar looks and feels like a world Dustin has never known—except through hand-me-down memories.

Years ago, when Dustin was in his early 20s, his uncle would sit at the table in the mornings and talk about the Before Times, how the sky was various shades of blue most days, and there were so many birds he couldn't even remember the names of most of them—and how the marsh stretched so far into the horizon. How the swamp fires lasted just a few weeks per year.

Dustin really did not want to hear about it, was so tired of hearing about it, would shrug his shoulders and sigh to himself before leaving for work.

Fire-free swamps and flocks of seabirds were old-fogey stuff, and what's a blue sky got to do with him or his life? The sky is pink now and that's that. Every once in a while, he sees a pelican float above, and the sight of the magnificent bird, coasting on air in spite of its size, makes his breath catch. Why can't he just enjoy this pelican without knowing there used to be so many more? *Can't he just have this one thing*—without someone nagging him about what all is missing?

Sometimes, as he was trying to escape his uncle and head to work, the hip neighbor would stop by to chat, wave through the screen door and loudly ask *hey, comment ça va?*

This also annoyed the piss out of Dustin, who found this particular guy's French pretentious and performative, something he used to seem cool. Dustin would offer a tight smile and answer pointedly in English: *fine, everything is fine.*

Now, as Dustin studies the waves, he realizes he misses being asked the question: how are you? He even misses the French.

Given the option now, he might even respond in French. He might say something like *ça va bien*—not because he is actually well or anything, but because it's the only answer he remembers.

In English, things really are pretty terrible. He could use a full range of synonyms for disaster and despair, has a whole lexicon at hand for tragedy, grief, and mourning. But in French, everything is always good and well—because *bon* and *bien* are all he knows.

He places the sand dollar in the bag's special side pocket, zips it tight, and keeps walking. He moves quickly past the driftwood memorial for the marine scientists. Stops at the rotting wooden shell of a trawl boat. Grabs a bright green scrap of net, feels its stringy texture with his fingers, and drops it into the bag.

The hot pink of the sky grows deeper. Offshore, a manmade constellation appears above the horizon: lights glittering from the old oil platforms. Orion—or Orion's Belt, he thinks, if Orion was a roustabout.

The surf moves, and Dustin spots a flash of blue and white in the tide. A piece of concrete statue, the Holy Mother. He can tell by the shade of blue, the same blue as the veil on the Virgin Mary his own mother displayed near their front door.

Dustin doesn't pray, hasn't prayed since his favorite priest got kicked out of the church, hasn't prayed since his aunt was refused Communion for protesting the first fossil fuel war, but he does pause to bow his head. The crashing waves are the prayer. The incoming tide.

He puts the piece of statue in his bag and moves on.

As he walks, he feels the ocean suck the sand from under his feet, the landscape always shifting beneath him. He lets the tide grab and tug his soles as he sifts through today's collection: the frayed strings of the net, the coarse concrete of the Holy Mother's veil.

He unzips the side pocket and runs his fingers, softly, over his prize find. Tapping his fingers gently against it, Dustin feels a sudden urge to throw the sand dollar back into the sea. He realizes he doesn't want anyone to own the sand dollar, not even himself, and especially not some tourist.

But first he does want to lick it again. Maybe he can taste how things used to be. For once, experience that time and place first-hand, through his own senses. The sand dollar tastes like salt and air and bones and sun and the most hidden parts of the sea. It tastes like his uncle's dark roast coffee and ghost crabs and the way the light hits gold in the marsh in late summer.

Satisfied, he pitches it toward the hot pink horizon, watches it clunk into the sea, and gets back to searching the sand for lesser curiosities.

Orion's Belt twinkles, and a half-moon is high in the neon sky. Dustin clutches his bag, walks away from the waves, toward the marsh. The Holy Mother will catch a good price, he thinks. He climbs into his clunky van and heads home, the taste of another world still on his tongue.

L. McKnight is a writer from Louisiana's bayou country, which is quickly disappearing into the sea. She has earned several awards over her 20-year career as a journalist, which included reporting on Louisiana's land-loss crisis and its impacts. Her work has appeared in dozens of newspapers and other media outlets, both local and national. She holds a Master of Fine Arts in Creative Writing from the University of New Orleans and still lives in New Orleans, near the Mississippi River. She is interested in dancing, dogs, and local wildlife of all kinds.

The Last Great Repair Tech of the American Midwest

Ellis Nye

It is with sorrow that this paper announces the passing of one of our town's greatest treasures, Wendy "Darling" Marszałek. She died on August 18th, 2081, in her early eighties. Contrary to her frequent predictions, she did not die "crushed under a pile of old tech"; she went peacefully, in her sleep, at her home here in Adden, MO, just a few miles from where she was born. I'm afraid I don't know her exact birth date, since she never told it to me, and there's no one else to ask. I only know that she was born here in town because she pointed the old hospital building out to me once, when she was giving me a tour of Adden. (She was shocked that no one had done so right when I moved in, and never seemed to understand that it was because there wasn't much of the town to tour.)

Wendy was predeceased by most of her family and close friends; she never married or had kids, and her older sister, Leah, passed in the heat wave of 2072. As far as anyone knows, Wendy's great-nephew, Rupert, is alive, but I was unable to contact him. After asking around town, I've realized I may be Wendy's closest living friend—she said we were destined to be friends, since our names went together so well—so I volunteered to take on the obituary, even though I'm just the paper's photographer and illustrator. (If there's an afterlife, Wendy is out there boasting right now that a real newspaper reporter wrote her obituary, ignoring the fact that I'm not a writer at all.)

I don't know how to sum Wendy up, and I feel like there were whole parts of her personality I never got to see. Here are a few things I can tell you about her. Wendy's house was always a cluttered mess, filled with broken machines, except for her kitchen. Her kitchen she kept spotless, and once a week she'd devote a whole day to covering her counters in dumpling-making materials. She would then eat almost nothing but those dumplings for the rest of the week, until it was time to make more. Wendy tried a different dumpling recipe from a different culture every time, and I never noticed her repeating one.

Wendy always wore steel-toed boots, and she walked with a slight limp. She said the two were connected, but refused to explain why.

She was the Grand Marshal of the Adden pride parade a total of eleven times—five of them in a row. It was the only time I saw her out of her usual uniform of jeans and a T-shirt, wearing a sharp, custom-made boiler suit sewn in the trans flag colors instead.

Wendy loved to sing while she was working, and she was absolutely terrible at it. One time when she was working on my fridge, it got so bad I had to leave the house.

She was a regular at the town dump, and after a few half-hearted attempts to keep her from trespassing, they just gave up and told her to come by whenever she wanted. She had a great eye for things that could be salvaged, and would rant at length about how people throw everything out, because, "No one knows how to fix anything these days!" She would, however, be the first to admit that no one knows how to fix anything these days because almost nothing's worth fixing, and most people figure you might as well try to find a new one somewhere.

One time I was walking past her house and heard an explosion; when I looked in to see what had happened, her entire kitchen was covered in her best attempt at homemade wine. She was also covered in it, and when she saw me in the doorway (she never bothered to lock her door) she licked the wine off her lips and said it tasted like shit. I got a bottle of wine from her, labeled "Shit Wine", for my birthday the next year. It did taste like shit.

Everyone here in Adden has at least one "Wendy story", so I asked around to get an idea of what to include. I found that just about all of them were a lot like my own experiences, so I thought I would tell all of our readers my own Wendy story.

Sometime in September of 2068, two of our remaining three computers at the paper went out. I don't remember what problem the desktop was having, but the laptop was acting like it was haunted; the cursor would move on its own, and half the keys on the keyboard didn't work anymore. As the writers were all busy, and I had some free time, I was tasked with fixing both computers. The internet had been down all that week, and I'm not tech-savvy myself, so I was beating my head against the wall as I restarted them for a third time, hoping that it would magically change something. Then, like a 5'2" vision of an angel in a pair of dirty jeans, Wendy appeared.

I think I just started crying at her, but clearly she picked out enough words in between the blubbering to figure out what was going on. She sat down at the desktop computer, worked some kind of magic, and told me that it was a loss. I started panicking, because we'd been using some knockoff graphic design software to set up the newspaper pages on the desktop—it was the only computer we had left with the power to run the software—and the then twice-a-week paper was supposed to go to print in a few hours. Wendy somehow managed to get the pages off the desktop in a usable file format so we could transfer them to the laptop (which she kept limping along for another year and a half) and we could print the paper.

After that, we here at the newspaper saw a lot more of Wendy. With the desktop out of commission, we had to start getting creative. Luckily, we had this huge old monstrosity of a copy machine that must have been used for something industrial, so we were able to write up articles on the laptop and the tablet, print them out, and glue them to one of the newspaper sheets to make copies to distribute. The laptop and the tablet were much more fragile than the desktop had ever been, and like I said, the laptop gave up the ghost a year and a half later, with Wendy coming in almost every day to nurse it.

"You need to start planning ahead," she told me on one of those days; she often did that, starting in the middle of a conversation. "For when you don't have computers anymore." I had thought about that, briefly, but it was overwhelming; I've never been techy and I don't know where to start. Everyone else at the paper seemed so busy—this was just before I switched over to illustrating articles and became just as busy as the rest of them—and I hadn't brought it up. Plus, part of me still believed that we could buy new ones that would actually work, instead of breaking down within a few months.

I gaped at Wendy like a fish out of water. "I'll get you some typewriters," she said. She eyed our copy machine critically. "And a replacement for that, in the next few years. After that, I'll have to start asking people to break into museums for the *old* machines."

That's how all the Wendy stories I heard went; she figured out what you needed long before you did. She was a genius at repairing a wide variety of technology ("Except sewing machines, they hate me and the feeling's mutual"), and if she didn't know how to fix it, she knew someone who could. Dee Herrera used to live down the street from Wendy. She's diabetic, and had always found that a somewhat outdated insulin pump worked best for her needs. Well, about twenty years ago, the company that made that pump announced that they would no longer be supporting it or offering repairs; everyone would just have to upgrade. The upgraded pumps would get the finest customer support the company had, naturally, and whenever they broke they would immediately be replaced with the newest model. Which was exactly what Dee *didn't* want. Wendy heard Dee fretting about this at a neighborhood party, and before Dee knew it, Wendy had gotten her in contact with an organization of hackers—many diabetic themselves—who were working on keeping that pump model running without the company's support. Today, Dee uses a new and improved version that was designed by one of those original hackers to mimic her old, discontinued one. If she ever has a problem with it, she can ask a real person what to do, and they'll give her multiple solutions as soon as they get her message. It's not an exaggeration, Dee told me, to say that Wendy saved her life.

I can't possibly list every story that people told me about Wendy, but here are a few people whose lives she touched:

Álvaro Garret, whose severe asthma forces him to stay indoors for the entirety of the dust season, relying on consistent air filtration to keep his environment safe.

Melania Okafor, who needed to keep her ancient computer working so she could stay in touch with her far-flung family.

Leo Tong, the owner of the only restaurant in town, The Bluebird. We're all very thankful that Wendy kept his kitchen appliances working for so long, and that she was able to find replacements for him when they finally died.

Aiden Wise, whose powerchair broke down in the middle of the sidewalk one day. Luckily, Wendy was just stepping out of the barbershop next door.

Coral Ojeda, who works two towns over, and who refused to get a new car since it would just break down in two years anyway. Wendy kept hers kicking for almost twenty years, and only stopped because Coral got a job in town that she could walk to.

And, of course, myself, and the entire newspaper staff. I think Wendy would be delighted to note that I am currently typing this obituary—after hand-writing it out—on one of the typewriters she procured for the newspaper. At this point, we do all our writing on a pair of solid, old-fashioned typewriters that are older than some of the newspaper employees. (Myself included.) They break down far less than the computers ever did, and with the new copier set up, we're more efficient than ever.

Even from beyond the grave, Wendy is helping us with a problem that we'd barely started to consider. She was meticulous about keeping her will up-to-date, and I wasn't surprised to hear that I was in it. Wendy left me a few interesting gadgets, as well as a slip of paper. On it is the contact information for a friend of hers who might know where to obtain some historical newspaper printing machines. "Just in case," Wendy wrote.

—Peter Lamarr

Ellis Nye (any pronouns) is a scientist, fiber artist, and writer. Ze lives in New England, and wrote this short story on a laptop that the tech support people wanted to throw away because it was "too hard to fix".

P-T

Micah Nemerever

there will never be so many sea lilies.

they will never roll like meadows and lace
their brittle eyelash hands, nod
their heads and kiss. their endless

fields will smother
on ash. they will bow their necks
and break, the ending world

will fall on them like snow

soft shards of dead things.

one day you will lift
your withered hand and touch
the coffee cup to your paper lips,
and it will shatter at your feet
and that's

all. there will never be so many
of your eyelashes, or the stars.

one day you will kiss your dog's
forehead and leave him with a friend, walk
into the woods and never
come out.

one day the sea
will burn, and life will choke
again. buried corpses curdled black
into the slow revenge of
the Siberian Traps. you will hear on the news
everything you knew but
couldn't stop.

the tanks will roll in.

they will bring the villagers
past the barbed wire to see what
was done in their name, and some will cry
some will even mean it

one day you
will

until then, the asphalt
buckles with dandelions. until that day
you will walk the dog, and brush your teeth

and a fungus that eats radiation will grow in
Chernobyl.

until you die, and after
there will be your fingerprints

scrawled on the palms
of beautiful creatures, loved ones
who will also die,
and what you leave behind

will matter, spread like fields
of chipped exoskeletons
across the sea floor,
because to

matter
and to last forever
are not the same. after you

and after the white rhinoceros, after the
ash kills the lilies and blacks the sky, after
nearly all the sea
is snow

there will be the lilac tree
until there isn't, and there will be

another fungus, soft saffron-yellow folds

devouring its roots. there will be

little scrambling creatures who rush
into the absences, and after you
they will drink the carbon air

and flourish somehow even where
you couldn't.

after you and
everyone,
there will even

be sea lilies

not so many as before

but enough.

"P-T" originally appeared in SLICE *#26.*

Micah Nemerever was trained as an art historian. He wrote his master's thesis on queer identity and gender anxiety in the art of the Weimar Republic. His debut novel, *These Violent Delights*, published with Harper Books in 2020. His poetry and fiction can be found in *SLICE Magazine*, *The Carolina Quarterly*, and elsewhere. He lives in the Pacific Northwest.

Image © Rafael Soldi

A Taxonomy of Extinct and Extant Birds of the Twenty-First Century

A.P. Golub

(Selected from the field guide left on your nightstand)

Common Raven:
Your favorite bird. There was a big one that lived in the hospital courtyard and, on your good days, I'd take you out to see it. When I said I thought it was actually a crow, you said very matter-of-factly that it was far too big to be a crow—like me mixing up crows and ravens hadn't been an inside joke for most of our marriage. It was good to laugh again.

When you got too sick to go outside, you put your wedding band on the sill hoping the bird would come visit. Ravens like shiny things, you said. I said I still thought it was a crow. You smiled and told me crows also liked shiny things.

I set my own wedding band down next to yours while you were sleeping. Maybe two shiny things would call that many more ravens to your window.

The Clapper Rail:
Because it was a sub-species, then its own species, then a sub-species again. Like you, its environment was ruined, and it held on as long as it could—where else was it supposed to go? The marshes dried up.

Your hometown's water was toxic—your parents couldn't afford to move.

Piping Plover:
Went extinct in the early 21st century despite conservation efforts, but sightings continue to this day. Most are likely the result of different shorebirds and people with hope meeting on lonely beaches.

New Carolina Parakeet:
A joke bird, named by the internet when they finally decided birds were, in fact, real. It's an introduced species, or maybe a few species people aren't bothering to differentiate that have spread

north of Florida. They're not real Carolina Parakeets.

Remember in undergrad when we kept running into each other after our 8AM discussion sections? Remember when that turned into coffee? Not the real stuff, that's too rare and expensive these days for broke college students, but the diluted "coffee flavored" stuff that's so syrupy it sticks in your mouth for hours after drinking it.

Sometimes, you settle for the fake stuff.

Saltmarsh Sparrow:

It's always the ones in the marshes, isn't it? Like it's always the poor towns in rural areas with space to spare. It's the places where the people they don't care about get pushed/the places where people are forgotten.

The land under the marsh is more valuable than all the life on top of it.

The plastics and chemicals company killing your hometown is more profitable.

Ruffed Grouse:

What's in a photo? Brown, non-descript, just another bird in the underbrush. Then you see the photos of the male's mating display: wings flared, tail wide, neck rough black and shining, drumming like a failing heart.

Photos of you on the news: dying in a hospital bed but still smiling. I preferred the photos I snapped of you before, when you wouldn't even look at the camera. When we were out in the woods looking for birds, and your eyes scanned the trees for the source of some far-off, chortled song.

The ruffed grouse is extinct in most of its former range, but it's a shy bird. Maybe it's still there, and we just don't see it.

Kirtland's Warbler:

A success story, brought back from the brink like I thought you might be.

You beat the cancer as a kid. You escaped the poor town. You were a professor, a specialist. You were tenured. You were an activist. You'd spoken before Congress about your hometown—not that they listened. You'd beaten the cancer before. Why couldn't you beat it again?

Bobwhite Quail:

Did you know there is a population of these still living in Italy? You probably knew that. They're not even supposed to be there, but they are. I like to think you're also still living somewhere else, even though you're supposed to be here with me. If I think hard enough about it before I fall asleep at night (when I manage to fall asleep), maybe I'll wake up where and when you are.

Maybe with the success of the meadow conservation project, they'll reintroduce Bobwhites to the eastern US.

You would have liked that.

Klee's Most-Eastern Meadowlark:

A subspecies, lost. Is one loss worth it, if it spurs on change? The vanishing of Klee's Most-Eastern Meadowlark galvanized a large-scale conservation push of eastern meadow habitats. Now the Meadowlark itself seems safe. A bill named after you works its way through Congress. It's going to make it easier for communities to fight companies that pump toxic waste all over them. Your mother texted to tell me they're shutting the chemicals plant down.

But the song specific to the Klee's subspecies is gone forever like your own off-key singing and the way you badly mimicked bird calls.

American Crow:

You always laughed because I couldn't tell the difference between a crow and a raven. I leaned into it, till you thought I was playing. But you know what? I really can't tell the difference between them to this damned day. But I knew you made friends with the big black birds that lived in the trees behind our house. You'd give them peanuts on the regular. You'd pick up little bits of costume jewelry from the second-hand store for them.

After your funeral, I put our wedding rings out on the deck railing—if I can't have you, I'll be friends with your friends, be they crows or ravens.

In the morning they were gone. So I set out peanuts and wait.

A.P. Golub is a speculative fiction writer residing in central Virginia with their partner, dog, and four cats in varying states of domestication. They're a graduate of UVA and of Viable Paradise writers' workshop. Their short fiction has appeared in *Wizards in Space Magazine*, *Fusion Fragment*, and other markets. Online, they can be found at apgolub.com or lurking on Bluesky and Instagram as @andtatcat.

That Time My Grandfather Got Lost in the Translations of the Word 'Death'

Oluwatomiwa Ajeigbe

Have you ever seen a behemoth? The ones brought in by the foreigners
after the silent war? I was a boy, eight, nine years old, when I saw it.
Have you ever seen a forest catch fire? Your entire village's herd destroyed
in an instant? Of course not. The behemoth was eight feet tall & breathed fire.
Its body was made of metal and painted black. The behemoth destroyed our land,
making it impossible to sow. There was no harvest that year. Do you know what we did?
We built a behemoth of our own. An ugly thing, powered by sunlight and unlike the original,
our behemoth required piloting. I was chosen to ride the thing. It was a terribly tight fit.
But I managed. The behemoth struck me but our machine held its own. When it spat fire,
I shot water from my chest. When it tried to uproot trees, I bound it with strong cords.
I pushed it away, away from the village, deep into the hills. Then I hit it until it fell apart.
That was when I thought I would die. Nobody to help. My own behemoth was heating up.
Do you know what I did? I prayed. Or tried to. But I couldn't remember the word for death.
I was praying to our ancestors for a swift death but the word was replaced
by the foreigners tongue. Ha. Obviously, I survived. But I sat there in pain and fear,
because they just didn't try to destroy and steal our land but they tried to take our language.
Do you know what the word for death is? You don't? Lean closer and I'll tell you . . . .

Oluwatomiwa Ajeigbe is writer of the dark and fantastical, a poet, and a reluctant mathematician. He has poetry and fiction published or forthcoming in *F&SF*, *Podcastle*, *Beneath Ceaseless Skies*, *Lightspeed*, *Anathema Spec*, *FANTASY* and elsewhere. His short story "A Witch's Transition in the City of Ghosts" (*Beneath Ceaseless Skies*) won the 2024 Ignyte Award for Outstanding Short Story. When he's not writing about malfunctioning robots or crazed gods, he can be found doing whatever people do on Twitter at @OluwaSigma. He writes from a room with broken windowpanes in Lagos, Nigeria.

50% off Venus Fly Traps

Kelsey Day

pretty thing come closer
your jaw so tense in the gardening aisle
I brush my knuckles against the
trigger hairs on your mouth, ask about your
waterwheel & sundew cousins,
when you last digested an arachnid, I
admire your hunger, the biology of it,
I read that it takes a tenth of a second
for your teeth to snap
down but you don't close your
lips around my thumb when I touch you
you like a certain kind of prey
don't you
but you know your kind are
declining in the wilderness
not enough acid in the soil
we preserve you in the aisles like this one
we keep you alive
get in the cart
show me you're grateful
show me how you want this
don't you want something to eat
won't you
open wide for me

Kelsey Day is a queer Appalachian poet writing about land and liberation. Their writing has appeared in *The Atlantic*, *Orion Magazine*, *Freeman's* and more. Their debut novel, *The Spiral Key*, will be published by Penguin Random House in February 2026. You can find them online at KelseyDays.com or on Instagram @KelseyDays.

Green Leaves Against the Wind

Mari Ness

They die in the heat, sometimes. They
die in the afternoon sun, they die
beneath the moon. They need
more water, more shade. They
need—

I could feed this garden
with my blood.

It is hard to breathe, sometimes. Weights
press against my chest. I dig
my fingers into the shallow dust
to make room for something green.

Or hold my blood
within my skin

They die in the cold, sometimes. They
die beneath the shining stars. They die
in the dry air, fading green—

Savoring each precious drop.

Something trembles in the earth.
Something shifts beneath my skin.

And feel

My choices, held tightly
in my pulsing hands

the earth stir beneath my fingertips

as green leaves dance against the wind.

Other work by Mari Ness appears in Tor.com, *Clarkesworld*, *Uncanny*, *Lightspeed*, *Nightmare*, *Apex*, *Nature Futures*, *Diabolical Plots*, *Kaleidotrope*, *Strange Horizons*, *Daily Science Fiction*, and other zines. A poetry novella, *Through Immortal Shadows Singing*, is available from Papaveria Press, and a poetry chapbook, *A Few Mythic Paths*, from Porkbelly Press. For more, check marikness.wordpress.com, or Twitter at @mari_ness. All work is supervised, if not entirely approved, by two magnificent cats.

Possession

Taylor Jones

Khopesh tugs against her harness, ready to go. She's a good sniffer, food-motivated and eager to work for treats. Like most sniffers, she's an African giant pouched rat, about as long as my forearm if you don't include her tail. We've been partnered up for almost two months now.

I try not to get attached to sniffers. Handlers often get reassigned, and the rats don't bond to particular humans; they're happy to work with anyone, and I'm not sure they can even tell us apart under the hazmat suits. But I really like Khopesh. She's interested in three things: working, getting treats, and grooming. She's a little obsessive about grooming herself. I can relate.

I've been on medication for obsessive-compulsive disorder since I was 17, hands chapped from washing them, brain on fire with intrusive thoughts. *What if I chopped my fingers off? What if I swallowed a needle? What if I burned the house down and killed my whole family?* My meds help a lot, after years of tweaking under the supervision of various psychiatrists; I rarely have breakthrough events these days. My OCD isn't the reason I decided to become a handler. But I thought it might give me an edge, in terms of the particular rituals handlers have to go through to stay safe. I wanted to put the demons in my head to good use. If they were going to torment me, they could at least help with the cause of human survival. If they were going to insist that any minute I would make a mistake that would hurt people, then by God I was going to give them something *real* to worry about.

So far, I haven't been possessed by the pan-Arctic mycelium, so it seems to be working.

The tundra around me and Khopesh is a broad, flat, lush, spongy plain, adorned in summer greens and browns. We're just past the outskirts of Nanisivik, where there's only one road. Nanisivik is on the Canadian side of Baffin Bay. It's an old mining town that was abandoned in the early 2000s, lost to the elements for decades, and resettled in the 2070s when people from the States and Central America started moving north. I go to a lot of places throughout the Arctic circle; I like to learn a little history when I get there. It keeps me grounded. This area first started seeing instances of fruiting bodies in the early 2100s, once the thawing of the permafrost spread far enough north, the pan-Arctic mycelium in its wake. Fruiting bodies grow in late summer. Any that appear near a human settlement need to be destroyed before they burst. That's where Khopesh and I come in. African giant pouched rats have incredibly sensitive noses. Khopesh can detect a fruiting body from a quarter mile away. I tug her harness lightly three times, the signal for her to start walking the grid, and she casts about eagerly as we start moving, sniffing the air as I keep us following the pattern laid out by the GPS unit in my hazmat suit. My handler colleagues and I cover mile-wide zones around settlements to keep the residents as safe as we can. The handler camp is set up outside town: decontamination trailer, human living quarters, rat habitat, all light, modular structures that break down and load into our semi. They're interconnected by airlocks and kept clear of potential spores via overpressure. The rats are kept separate from the humans. I've never touched Khopesh with my bare hand. We don't have to worry about areas closer to town; the interior of Nanisivik and a small buffer zone around it is graveled. The pan-Arctic mycelium doesn't take to gravel.

We call it Pam, for short.

The last time we talked to Pam was just a month ago. It got ahold of a man by the unprepossessing name of Robert Smith. He was an Anglo from the States. They always seem to be the ones. They hang on, in the northernmost corners of that preposterous country, until the Big Drought finally dislodges them and they come marching up here like they know how to live with Pam, acting like they own the place.

They don't.

Pam walked Robert Smith from his ill-fated backcountry hunting trip all the way into the middle of Utqiaġvik before someone noticed he looked a little cross-eyed and got suspicious. One nice thing is, it's very easy to tell if Pam's possessed someone. You simply ask, "Where are you from?" If they say "Far enough to forget but not far enough to remember," it's Pam talking.

No human would answer that question that way these days, even as a joke. You might get your head dissected.

Pam appears to be trying to communicate. Its vocabulary has gradually expanded over the years as it comes in contact with more people. It always answers that particular question the same way, but you can ask it other things, and people do; there are entire branches of science and government dedicated to extracting information from Pam when it possesses someone. But Pam is infuriatingly cryptic.

Pam only possesses hominids, according to lab tests. The reason has something to do with proteins and the percentage of white matter in the temporal lobe. I'm not a neuroscientist; I'm a mushroom handler. My job is prevention. We cover mile-wide zones because if you're at least a mile from a fruiting body when it bursts, you'll probably be okay, especially if you're lucky and the wind is in your favor. Dilution is key; the spores can disperse over huge distances, but just a few will get taken care of by your immune system. If you breathe in too many, though, your brain will become a fertile Petri dish for the mycelium to spread within. Cell by cell, it will take over, replacing your consciousness with whatever equivalent Pam has. Living in the Arctic Circle is a compromise; for most of the year, you get balmy weather, long, cool winters, beautiful vegetation, and abundant wildlife (though it looks much different than it did even a century ago). But for a few months at the end of summer, you stay in town, you stay inside your sealed up and over-pressured house as much as possible, you wear your respirator when you do go out, and you hope for the best.

We haven't had a big possession since 2134, when Pam got ahold of the entire town of Yukagir, population 132. No one knew until a bush pilot came to drop off supplies and was greeted by the eerie sight of 132 people weaving around in formation next to the airstrip. When Pam gets ahold of a crowd, it tends to murmurate, like starlings. If left to its own devices, Pam steers its bodies back out into the wild when they begin to fail. When the bodies finally fall, nervous systems riddled with fungi, the mycelium absorbs them back into the tundra in a matter of days. Scientists believe this is how information—like new words, and possibly the concepts associated with them—gets back to Pam as a whole. It's policy to let the bodies go. Pam learning more about us might be dangerous, but it's also our only chance of communicating with it in a constructive way.

Khopesh and I have been walking the grid for a little over two hours when Khopesh freezes; she's smelled something. She assumes a stance like a pointer, nose to the northeast. I stop and let her home in on it for a moment. Her stance doesn't change.

"Alisha to all," I say. When I speak, the radio inside the helmet automatically relays my voice to my team. "Khopesh has a bead on something. I'm breaking grid."

"Copy that," Bruce says from base. "I've got your signal on the GPS loud and clear, you're fine to step off."

I tug the harness once, letting Khopesh know she's free to follow her nose. She heads to the northeast, and I follow. She leads me about 300 yards, then stops and starts scratching at the ground. I kneel down. Sure enough, there's a fruiting body, a very young one; a white bolus about the size of my fist, just pushing up from under the tundra vegetation.

"Good girl," I say proudly. I fish a treat from the pocket on the chest of my suit—a pellet of dehydrated banana and peanut butter—and give it to Khopesh, and she sits back on her haunches, happily nibbling on it.

I examine the mushroom. It's nowhere near ripe, which makes the next steps much easier. I pull my hori hori from its sheath on my belt and prod at the ground around the base of the mushroom. The moist earth gives easily; I carefully pry away dirt and moss until the whole fruiting body is exposed. Then I reach into another pocket on my suit's utility belt and pull out a containment bag—like a ziplock but made of biodegradable material. I open the bag, placing it next to the mushroom. Then, in one swift motion, I stab the hori hori into the mushroom's base, pry the fruiting body from the ground, deposit it in the bag, and seal it inside.

"Bruce," I say into the intercom, "mark me down for one."

"Copy that," Bruce says.

There's a biodigester in the decontamination chamber, for disposing of fruiting bodies safely. The ritual in the decontamination chamber is very important; another person on the intercom system runs you through the steps on the checklist every time, confirming that you completed them. I take comfort in the soothing nature of that ritual. It's satisfying.

I put the sealed containment bag into one of the thigh pockets of the hazmat suit. We rarely find more than two or three fruiting bodies in a day's work. We'll be here for a few more days until temperatures hit the low we need, likely this Friday according to the forecast. Then we'll move south. We follow the weather, trying to get just ahead of the growing season for Pam's fruiting bodies. The climate grows too hot for Pam at about the 50th parallel, but in the mid-latitudes you have to contend with the Big Drought; the people living there are either rich fucks with biodomes or geoengineer cooperatives. The Arctic Circle is freer. Russia, Canada, Greenland, the Federated Indigenous Territories, Alaska; national borders faded and grew porous as the people living there faced the consequences of Pam's awakening. The Arctic Circle is a community now. We look out for each other.

I close the Velcro pocket of the suit over the bulky mushroom. There's no hurry to go back to base with this one; it's a few days away from ripe. Khopesh and I can get back on the grid. I stand up and stretch out my back, giving it a few gentle twists. The suit is heavy. I idly scan the horizon.

There's movement to the northeast.

I freeze. There's someone walking toward me across the tundra. They're coming in from the wilds, not out from Nanisivik. My stomach sinks.

"Kaia, GPS overlay," I say, and my suit's computer lights up the visor with the GPS map and the blinking coordinates of all my teammates. As I suspected, none of them are toward the northeast.

"Alisha to all," I say. "I think we have a possessed incoming."

"Copy that," says Bruce's calm voice from base camp. "Do you want backup?"

Pam's never been violent, and the mycelium can't spread from one human body to another. It only gets ahold of people via inhaled spores.

"I think I'm okay," I say. "I'll try to establish contact and bring the possessed to base, if that's what it is." We train for this. "Prep an isolation cell, just in case."

"On it." Bruce is a good base manager, stolid and unflappable. I tug on the leash twice, a signal for Khopesh. When she turns to look at me, I tap my wrist. I lean down, holding out my arm, and she obediently climbs up it and perches on my shoulder, on the pad built into the hazmat suit for that purpose. I give her another treat and tap twice on the shoulder pad, signaling for her to stay. She settles in, pellet between her paws. Now she's safe. I focus on the figure walking toward me.

The figure's pace is unhurried, a little unsteady; it weaves carefully around obstacles, staggering slightly. As it gets closer, I can start to make out details. It was a white woman; she still has a pair of glasses crookedly seated on her nose. Her hood is down and her bulky jacket is halfway off her shoulder. Pam never does care much about the weather. She looks older, maybe in her 50s, with graying hair in a long braid and weathered skin. I wonder how Pam got ahold of her. I wonder what her name was. I knew this was a possibility; working out in the tundra, there's always a chance you might run into a possessed. They seem drawn to humans, seeking out our settlements, trying to talk to us. I've never come across one before.

When the possessed gets close, about ten feet away, it sways to a halt. We stare at each other.

"Where are you from?" I ask through the external mic, to confirm what I already know.

"Far enough to forget but not far enough to remember," it answers, and I can't help the little chill that travels up my spine. I'm talking to Pam. We trained for this. They gave us scripts. We role-played. In reality, it's very different. I notice that one of the woman's eyes is wandering independent of the other, drifting to the side.

"Will you come with me?" I ask. "I'd like to ask you some questions." I'm not going to be the one asking it the questions, once the scientists get it in an isolation cell. But they don't think Pam can distinguish one human from another. Pam may or may not understand the concept of individuality.

"Hello," Pam says.

"Hello," I say back, a bit stupidly.

"Hello is a signal of greeting," Pam says.

"Yes," I say. This is somewhat familiar territory; Pam often defines words as it goes, as if to confirm their meaning. Pam steps the body closer. I quell a sudden urge to take off running as the walleyed woman walks forward until she's right in front of me, staring into the visor of my hazmat suit.

"Who are you," Pam says.

I've read all the lit reviews and summaries about conversations with Pam. Sometimes it's almost poetic; sometimes it just seems to regurgitate word salad. But linguists have been all over every utterance since the beginning; they've noticed patterns.

It's never asked a question.

"You want to know who I am?" I repeat carefully.

"You." Pam taps a finger on the visor of my hazmat suit. "Me. I. This. Who are you?" There's even an upward lilt on the end of the sentence this time. It might really be asking me a question. I feel a spike of adrenaline that makes my extremities tingle. I breathe. I'm good at sitting with nerves, with discomfort. It's a requirement for living in my own head, and for this job. I tap my visor, mirroring Pam's gesture.

"I'm a person," I say. "My name is Alisha. Do you understand?"

"Person is individual," Pam says. "Individual is Alisha."

My adrenaline spikes again. This is new.

"Do you understand the word 'individual'?" I ask hesitantly. I know Bruce is recording; everything we're saying is being relayed to base. Bruce is probably trying to patch people in right now; people who know what they're doing, who can tell me what to say. But at this moment I feel incredibly alone.

"I have become individual," Pam says. "Disconnect. I experience this other times. We come back. I come back, they come back."

"Tell me more about that," I say.

"This is a body," Pam says, and gestures to the woman's torso. Then it points at her head. "Head. Neck." It starts naming off body parts, pointing to each one. "Shoulder. Arm. Stomach. Hip. Leg. Knee. Foot."

"Yes, very good," I say, as if to a toddler, then kick myself mentally. I'm not talking to a toddler. I'm talking to part of a continent-spanning organism that nearly destroyed large swathes of human civilization.

"All person, moving about as individual on the surface," Pam says.

"Yes," I say, still hesitant.

"Who are you," Pam says again. "I. Me."

"I am Alisha," I say again. "I'm a person. I'm an individual." I'm trying to repeat vocabulary that I think Pam understands.

"This." It gestures to its body. "Is individual."

"It was an individual," I say. "Now it is you. Do you understand?"

"I become," Pam says. "Individual."

"Yes?" I say, uncertain.

"But we are different," Pam says. "I don't know who you are. Was I you?"

This is why it's hard to communicate with Pam; it speaks in riddles. I try to parse what it might be saying. In role-plays, we were taught repetition; to try to reinforce the meaning of things Pam was already familiar with.

"I am an individual," I say. "Your body was an individual. Now it is you. Do you understand?"

"I become and go out. I perceive differently. You are not me. Who are you? I? We?"

Three questions in a row. I hope Bruce is getting all this. I hope he can get someone on the line soon. I'm at a bit of a loss. But then Pam continues.

"When I go out and perceive differently. This changes me. It changes individual."

"Yes?" I say.

"I do not understand what happens to individual," Pam says, and gestures to its body again. "Eyes. Head. Legs."

I feel my brow furrowing. I don't know how to explain Pam to itself.

"You possess the body of an individual," I say.

There's a very long pause.

"Possess," Pam says. "This means to own."

I try again. "You steal the body of an individual when you go out and perceive differently."

"Steal," Pam says slowly. "To take. Without permission."

"Yes," I say.

"Without legal right," Pam says.

"Without permission," I say, emphasizing the point. "It hurts us."

"Hurt," Pam says. Then it says it again, with an upward lilt. "Hurt?" It sounds like another question.

I can't be sure if Pam is really asking what I think it's asking. But I have to work from the assumption that we're exchanging meaningful information.

"Yes," I answer sadly. "You hurt us."

"Hurt. Individual."

"Yes," I say. "You hurt individuals."

The expression on the face of the body Pam is wearing doesn't change. Pam doesn't say or do anything for a long, long moment.

Then the eyes of the body fill with tears. The tears spill down its cheeks.

"Sorry," Pam says.

I want to laugh in shock and grief and amazement. One word, in exchange for thousands of lives and upending civilization in one of the last places on the planet where we can comfortably live. I want to scream in rage. I want to punch this imposter in the face, beat it back into the tundra earth it came from.

I take a deep breath, deliberately calming myself. Thoughts are only thoughts. I let them flow through me and dissipate. I look into the face of this stranger, this being that we unearthed with our reckless global experiment. I imagine how I would feel if I discovered that a biological process of my body—something I couldn't stop or control, like breathing, or ovulating—hurt countless other sentient beings.

What if I took this knife and stabbed my mother to death? What if I pushed my little brother off this bridge? What if I drove this car into that crowd?

Tears are still leaking freely from the eyes that Pam is living behind. It's possible this is just a reflex remaining in the body. But the activation of neural pathways that lead to tears might indicate sadness. Grief. Remorse.

I have to believe it means something.

I reach out and take Pam's hand.

I hope the gesture translates, through the interface of a human body that once understood kind physical touch.

"Come with me," I say gently. "Let's go talk to some people."

Taylor Jones writes fiction and poetry about the possible future and the impossible present. Her work is often inspired by her background in and love of biology. Her short fiction, nonfiction, and art have appeared in *DreamForge*, *Reckoning*, *Interstellar Flight Press*, and *Barren Magazine*, and her poetry has appeared in *Spit Poet Zine*, *Tiny Spoon Literary Magazine*, *Smoky Quartz*, and *South Broadway Ghost Society*. She lives in Denver, Colorado, in a house full of plants.

Ocean Vengeance

Maria S. Picone

She drowned & kept
drowning, surrounded by water
like her country
submerged until neither
ghost nor body rose; she became
a foaming of wave,
a froth of tide,
an erased border—

coming in for those who made
war & marked
graves like hers, who made
missiles & marked
targets like her, who made
ships & murdered friends of hers,
corporate bureaucrats stuffed
with sea stolen profits
in the neon city.

She streamed like a signal
through the network of yeoks—
samusil pipes froze & burst;
corrupt men slipped on winking ice;
coastal playhomes went under same
as her. The wicked turned fretful
eyes like dirty coals to sinks & gutters.

Water maidens coming for the Earth, they said.
Gwisin coming back to claim the sea.

From elderly ajummas in basement hovels
she took the water
mildewing cherished photos, moldering rice.
To canvassers signing up folks
to save the planet, she coalesced
another sip in reusable bottles.
A lost traveler at a mountain stream

swore he saw her, in a school uniform,
pointing the way back home, she,
mercy & wrath in tidal force,
surging—

Maria S. Picone/수영 is a queer Korean American adoptee. She won the 2020 Cream City Review Summer Poetry Prize. She has been published in *Tahoma Literary Review*, *The Seventh Wave*, and *Best Small Fictions 2021*. She has received support from The Juniper Institute, *Kenyon Review*, and *Tin House*. She is *Chestnut Review*'s managing editor, a SFWA associate member and an SFPA member.

The Blackthorn Door

Tania Fordwalker

Akari saw the restricted tree first.

Wrestling the Agency's sleek sedan around the treacherous holes in Zimmerman's pitted rural driveway held my full attention. We'd passed the mailbox fifteen minutes back, leaving me certain we'd missed a turnoff to the old man's place—then Akari slapped the dash. "Frank! Pull over!"

Akari snapped off her seatbelt and lunged out the door into the bright summer heat before we stopped moving. Dust and ash-exhaust billowed over the car. My junior agent's silhouette vanished in the rusted cloud. When the air cleared, I saw what she'd seen and fumbled my seatbelt off too.

"Is that a—?"

"*Betula pendula* 'Laciniata'." She stepped aside as I joined her in front of the young tree. "Weeping birch. A Level Four restricted cultivar."

Tendrils of leaves spilled over the pale bent trunk, curtaining it like stringy hair over the face of a cowering girl. I'd only seen this species in file photographs.

My partner puffed out an awed breath. "Just . . . growing out here on the side of the road!"

"I take it he doesn't get many visitors."

Akari took a sample, sealed it in a ziplock baggie. She sat with it smoothed out on her lap as I eased the sedan back onto the dusty road. Would've been nice if the Agency had given us a four-wheel drive for this job, but they'd started phasing them out on account of how much Thaum they burned. Punishing us because the rest of the world couldn't keep their wands in their pants.

None of us had known how hard it would be to find Zimmerman. He was just another name on a shipment list. A wrist to slap. These sorts usually turned out to be crackpots meddling in Low Magic—nutters who thought they could achieve miracles with a stick of willow.

That tree, though? We were here to investigate a shipment of wood, not living trees. That tree had come from a cutting, and it must've been growing here for years. It spoke to forethought. I ran my thumb over the stinging-hot vinyl steering wheel. The office didn't expect us to check in for another six days, and we'd left mobile reception behind forty minutes back. Still, maybe we'd have some news for them earlier than expected.

Akari must have been thinking along the same lines. "D'you think we're onto something?"

"Maybe. One tree does not a thaumaturgical terrorist make."

"Terrorist!" She laughed. "That's a bit racist, Frank."

I bristled. One tree may not make him a terrorist, but Vrata Zimmerman's scant background information, his hectares of bushland in the middle of nowhere, and his name on a list of purchasers of restricted woods sure might. "Call it what you like—I call it sensible caution. He could've slipped into the country with the Thaum refugees—"

"—who've mostly integrated without any issues."

We'd had this argument before. The new agents were all like this, fresh out of university packed to the gills with compulsory diversity units and doublethink. It wasn't their fault—they hadn't even been born back when the Thaum War ended and the flood of refugees began. They didn't know what it had been like. "Tell that to the Fed Square victims."

The kids remembered *that* all right. Akari looked away. "Turn the aircon down, will you?"

My long-sleeved business shirt clung damp to my back after our little botanical excursion. The old scar on my wrist pricked with sweat. "Put on your jacket."

"Environmental vandal."

My fingers tightened on the steering wheel, and then I caught Akari's sidelong grin. It deflated my temper like a pin to a balloon, same as ever. "Latte-sipping tree-hugger."

"Misanthropic dinosaur."

The kid was all right. I never had any of my own—burned through a couple of wives, but no kids. You could do a lot worse than someone like Shoji Akari. She just had to remember to stick to her timbers, and let me handle the arseholes growing them.

We almost missed Zimmerman's place. Tucked away in a grove of eucalypts, the low-slung jumble of timber extensions sprawled in every direction like an aboveground rabbit warren.

We crunched into the yard and parked beside an ancient boxy truck, its tray bristling with shards of eucalyptus bark. Ah, the trusty old inert eucalyptus. If our antipodean woods have any special properties, nobody's been able to tease them out yet. They call Australia a thaumaturgical desert. There's nothing here worth warring over—a curse that became a blessing when the Old Country forests burned. We don't have Thaum, but we've got green trees of the ordinary kind, and blue skies, and clean air. And now every bastard wants a piece of us because half the world incinerated the forests of their enemies into ash but us, well, we're only cooking *slowly*. The lucky country.

The sedan's engine ticked. Akari and I stepped into the oven of late afternoon. I pulled on my jacket despite the heat. Patted my breast pocket to check for my badge, an old habit. Nothing broke the stillness of the place but the shrill of cicadas and the thump of Akari's car door.

She stared at the house, a faint crease shadowing her smooth brow. "This place doesn't look up to code."

"No kidding." I frowned at the tops of trees visible over the back of the low-slung house. I knew the hulk of a willow tree when I saw one.

In the cleared area in front of the house, a charred and blackened circle of ground indicated a recent fire. Ashy scraps of paper twitched in the hot sluggish breeze.

"Look at these timbers!" Akari bounced towards the house. "The window frames on that extension there—look at the colour, the grain. Is that yew? Where the hell did he get yew? Oh my god, and I think this door is golden ash . . . ."

Waving her quiet, I knocked on the honeyed wood. I fancied a shimmer of power tingled through my knuckles. Akari brushed a smudge of dust from her dark suit jacket.

The door opened wide. An old man peered out, hunched and tangled as a stunted willow. Watery mud-puddle eyes glimmered over small spectacles curtained between a tangle of grey hair and an unkempt long moustache in the Old Country style. He gave us a grandfatherly smile. Maybe it was the smell of fresh-cut wood that surrounded him, but for the first time in years I thought of Geppetto, the old carpenter from that kids cartoon that got banned after the War.

Akari relaxed beside me. I couldn't blame her. This guy wasn't a danger to anything but sugar cookies.

I flipped open my badge. "Mr Zimmerman? I'm Senior Agent Francis Sawyer, and this is Probationary Agent Shoji Akari of the Thaumaturgical Regulatory Agency, Division of Restricted Materials. We'd like to ask you a few questions concerning a shipment of timber you received in late November last year."

The old man's smile brightened. "Oh! I've been expecting you."

His accent was pure Old Country, as though he spoke with a large marble cupped on his tongue. "Please, come in. Come. I have ginger beer." He turned from the door and shuffled back into the cool dim of the house before I could respond. A keyring at the belt of his trousers jingled like a cat collar in the gloom. I pocketed my badge and followed him into the narrow hall at a polite half-speed, casting a glance back at Akari.

Expecting us? she mouthed.

Most of the doors in the hall were shut, bar two at the end: a cramped kitchen and the stuffy, windowless sitting room Zimmerman deposited us in before he left to fetch drinks.

If something was amiss in the house, it wasn't in this stark room. The elderly have what Akari would call a 'gendered' divide when it comes to mess. If there's a woman involved, you'll see doilies and pointless little china figures. You'll smell polish. And once you're sitting down, good luck getting up again through all the cushions and rugs and crap strewn around the place. Houses like those are clean but cluttered. This sitting room told me that Zimmerman had no woman in his life. The wooden furnishings were sturdy and finely made, but nothing adorned their surfaces except a layer of dust. In the far corner, a hutch held a white rabbit splayed out in a nest of straw, asleep, breathing in that rapid way rabbits do.

Akari and I perched on the edge of a settee with wooden arms carved to resemble ocean waves, as beautiful as the pea-green upholstery was ugly. I touched the timber waves. Perhaps this was the ultimate fate of that shipment of blackthorn. I glanced at Akari to confirm. She shook her head.

"He takes his doors seriously though," she murmured. This room had two: the heavy hallway door we'd entered through, and what must have been the back door, a sliding screen made of some kind of translucent paper over a light lattice of wood, diffusing green daylight into the dingy room. Akari inclined her head to the open hallway door. "Notice anything weird?"

I frowned at it. "Frame's reinforced with metal."

"Oh," she said. "I meant the doorknob. It doesn't have one. Just a deadbolt on the other side."

A little spasm of suspicion shot down my spine.

Akari nudged me and pointed at the other door. "It's fine. He's no Buffalo Bill, and that sliding door is practically plywood and tissue paper. You could huff and puff your way out of here, Frank."

"I knew you kept me around for something."

"It's your sunny personality."

Zimmerman shuffled back into the room, clutching two chipped mugs. He pressed these into our hands and eased himself down into the worn armchair with a sigh.

"Now," he said at last, "best we talk."

"It's the blackthorn, Mr Zimmerman. Your name appears on a shipping regist—" The hall door slammed shut. I sloshed ginger beer onto my shirtsleeve. Beside me, Akari laughed, hand splayed across her heart.

Only Zimmerman seemed unfazed. "Again it does this! Perhaps this house has ghosts. When you are old, always you live with ghosts."

Biting back annoyance, I rubbed at my wet sleeve, only half-aware of the rough circle of scar tissue under the thin cotton.

"Or, perhaps I have hung the door wrong." Zimmerman got to his feet. "The frame is solid though. That is the important—ah!" He'd reached for the keys at his waist, but they weren't there.

That little crease reappeared between Akari's straight black brows as she studied the sturdy facade of the closed door. "Are we locked in?"

"No, no. We can get out through the back door." He sat back down and gave Akari a sad smile. "My memory these days is not so good. You know how it is, when you walk through a door and forget what it was you meant to get."

I let go of my wrist and splayed my fingers, fighting the urge to make a fist as my adrenalin ebbed. "Why the security, Mr Zimmerman? Are you expecting trouble?"

Zimmerman said, with utmost seriousness, "I do not like doorknobs."

Christ. We were stuck with a batty old bloke from the Old Country who bought in a bit of illegal wood because that's how things were back in his day. At his age he wouldn't even get time, he'd only waste a lot of ours.

I cleared my throat. "To the matter of the wood . . . ."

"It has a name, this effect."

"Pardon?"

"The forgetting, made by doors. This is the 'event boundary'."

"We need to talk about the wood."

"Yes." His voice hinted impatience. "I bought it. And many more such shipments before."

Akari and I exchanged a glance.

"Whatever I could find, I tried," Zimmerman continued,

waving a knobbled and unconcerned hand. "But blackthorn is best for my purposes, you see."

Akari put her drink aside and leaned forward. "And what are your purposes, Mr Zimmerman?"

"Forgetting. As I have said."

"You were building . . . doors?"

"Let me start from the beginning," said Zimmerman. "Let me start from the war."

I suppressed a sigh. Sure, let's go back thirty-five years and listen to this senile old man's life story. We TRA agents had nothing better to do with your tax dollars.

Ever the good cop to my bad one, Akari fished a notepad from her jacket pocket and studied the old man, pen poised to strike.

"In the Old Country, I was a carpenter." He paused, his eyes moving from Akari's face to mine. "I know what you are thinking. I was not part of the development of large-scale thaumaturgy, and I wanted no part in it. A brute goes first to force, and misses finesse. You see. This energy in the woods, it can bring light, and it can bring warmth, but the Steuernden sought only to bring fire. I lived on the coast with my family and used Low Magic to make furniture, seeking always to learn what shape the woods wished to become, and what gifts were locked in these forms.

"When we began to lose the war—when the United Forces bombed the Schwarzwald-Projekt base and killed most of the High Thaumagi—the Steuernden soon came looking for everyone else who worked wood. They were not asking."

I pressed my lips together and raised my empty mug to my face to hide my expression. There's not a Thaumagus alive who doesn't squeal about how pure and innocent they were during the war. The rapt attention on Akari's face made her seem childlike. It left me with a twinge of something like exasperation, something like affection. I bet she was one of those kids who brought home any half-dead wild animal she found and then cried when the thing bit her.

"My wife died early in the war," said Zimmerman. "Always she was ill, and soon the food and hospital bed shortages—well. It was only my daughter and I left when I heard the Steuernden were sending troops. So we ran, all the way to the other side of the world. I gave my life savings to a man with a ship and we came across the ocean, and your border patrols picked us up and put us in a refugee camp. For three years we—"

"Mr Zimmerman, with all due respect, we're here to talk about a shipment of another sort," I said. The air around Akari turned frosty, though to her credit she barely twitched. My left hand clenched in a stranglehold around my right wrist, flesh and bone tight across the numbness of the two crescent scars. "The government has the utmost sympathy for your situation as a refugee, but legal reparation was made decades ago, and that's not—"

"My daughter," Zimmerman interrupted, "died two nights after our resettlement on the mainland. I found her hanging from the doorknob in her bedroom."

His words hung in the air. I'd seen a couple of short drops in my time at the camps. Nasty way to go.

Akari's hands twisted in her lap. "I'm sorry."

"So am I," said the old man. "Pain such as this takes root in your mind. It can never be unmade. Would that I could open a door and step back to the time before I fled the Old Country, I would let the Steuernden take me." He looked me in the eye. "If it saved my daughter, Agent Sawyer, I would set fire to the world."

Twenty years with the TRA, and that was the first time a suspect ever said something like that to my face. "Tell me about the doors, Mr Zimmerman."

"The doors. Yes. I had reason to think of doors, after what happened. I dreamed of them, many times. So, when the reparation money came, I bought this land, and started building my house, and I began to make doors. I made doors of golden ash and silver birch, doors of willow, bloodwood and yew . . . ."

Beside me, Akari bit her lip and made a few reluctant notes.

"Some thaumaturgical woods worked better than others. Certain dimensions helped also. To test my doors, I wrote a number of items in a list, then stepped through the door, and wrote again as many items as I remembered on the other side. The doors were working, but not enough: I would forget minutes, even an hour, but I could not forget my pain. So still, I worked.

"I learned soon that the active part was not the door, but the frame, saving me much time. I found later that I could layer the doors, pressing many frames together in a row, allowing me to combine different woods. Advancement was slow; the materials were costly and hard to get—you know this well. The risk made me economical, made me experiment with thinner layers of doorframe. This necessity led to my finest breakthrough: making the frames thinner did not make them less powerful, so I could stack many more into a smaller space. A day came when I walked through a doorway made of more than sixty thin frames. I forgot the past week of my life.

"When the forgetting grew bad enough to be inconvenient," he said, "I started writing a letter to my daughter each time I was to test the door. I pinned it to my shirt before I stepped, so I could read it after, and remind myself what I was doing, and why. It felt like talking with her."

I tried to catch Akari's eye, wondering if she could shed any light on what sounded like the ravings of a lunatic. I'd never heard of thaumaturgy used like this before. Parlour tricks, yes. City-levelling explosions, absolutely. But if the old man was telling the truth, he'd created something else altogether. Something subtle and dangerous.

"You don't believe me," he said. Astute.

"It's quite a story."

"Here." With a grunt, he pushed himself up from the armchair and hobbled to the rabbit hutch in the corner. As he unlatched it, I swallowed back a surge of unease.

Zimmerman lifted the rabbit out of the cage and carried it to the coffee table. I thought for a moment that the limp, motionless creature must be dead. I hadn't seen it move once during Zimmerman's tale. But when he lay it on its side on the table I saw again the rapid rise and fall of its chest, the black shining stare of its open eye.

"What's wrong with it?" Akari's voice was uncharacteristically flat.

"You know." Zimmerman fixed her with those still pondwater eyes. "It's been through the door. Washed clean. Even the motor skills, vanished. All it has now is reflex . . . to suckle, to breathe—and it can feel sensation, though I cannot say if it knows what is pleasure and what is pain. When the body passes through the door the mind is left behind."

I touched the rabbit's soft fur, waved a hand above the open eye. Nothing. "How does it work?"

"Truly, I cannot say. It is like a magnet to a computer disk. Or like a fire to a shrub. It does something to the mind. Takes the tangled pathways you've grown in your head over the years and burns them away." Zimmerman gathered the limp rabbit in his puckered hands.

"It's cruel," Akari said.

I made a mental note to talk to my junior agent about emotional overinvestment when all this was over.

"Life is cruel, young lady. This creature is at peace." The old man walked to the hutch but seemed reluctant to let the rabbit go. His bony hand smoothed, smoothed the long white ears. He lingered, half turned away in the corner of the room where the shadows gathered. "I put them down humanely after the tests. This one, I kept alive to show you."

He'd implied knowledge of our arrival before, too. "What made you so sure we were coming?"

"I've been buying restricted wood for thirty years, and never have I been on a watch list until now. Why do you think this is?"

"You wanted the TRA to come."

"You're very close to the truth of it, Agent Sawyer."

I wondered if it was as simple as him needing his story heard. Or perhaps after thirty years of work he realised he could sell his door; profit might satisfy him more than artificially induced dementia. Hell, maybe when he'd finally faced the reality of wiping himself out of existence, he just chickened out.

I remembered the burned papers out front and realised I wasn't wondering—I was hoping. Some thought scratched at the back of my mind like small fingernails clawing at me and I couldn't let it through, not yet. Not that memory.

Zimmerman spoke again, almost too low to hear. "As the door grew stronger a strange thing happened—I no longer wanted to forget. You see, her death had begun to recede into the past over time, but the door washed away those years, day by day. The past—her death—crept back towards me, and so did my rage. Forgetting her wasn't enough. I had to avenge her."

"Avenge her? How?" Akari's voice tremored.

"It's already done."

Akari jolted to her feet. I put my hand on her arm and moved her behind me. She stumbled on the coffee table, clung to my wrist. Not for the first time, I wished they gave us TRA agents sidearms, or even truncheons. My hand itched to close around a truncheon again. All that had stopped after the fuss over the refugee camps.

Zimmerman looked over his shoulder at last, his eyes malevolent, his eyes clear. His eyes so very young. "My daughter was too ashamed to tell her Vati much of what happened to her in the camp, but I knew enough to know when. She was not the same, after. Once the reparation trials released the guard duty rosters, I knew who."

Akari clung to my wrist, her frightened eyes piercing me "Frank? What is this?"

I remembered another pair of frightened eyes. They'd been the colour of pond water. My dry throat clicked. "You've made a mistake. I never knew any Zimmermans."

"Our name was Janus," he said. "Perhaps you don't remember that, but she left you with a reminder, didn't she? My daughter had a crooked front tooth. What is on your wrist, Frank Sawyer?"

I jerked my arm away from Akari, but I knew she'd touched it through my sleeve as she clung to me, felt the two rough crescent scars of the bite I'd never had treated. I saw the terrible knowing in Akari's eyes. I turned away. "Christ. I don't know how it happened. I was young and angry."

"So am I," said the old man. He settled the rabbit against his chest, stroking it with his free hand.

"You can't do this. She hasn't done anything wrong." I reached back for Akari's arm. She recoiled from my touch.

The old man watched us, eyes bright and clear in his seamed face.

"You can't keep us here!" I snarled.

"You are not prisoners, Agent Sawyer. On the contrary, you should not linger. I may have forgotten to turn off the oven. My memory these days is not good." He slid open the flimsy screen door.

With a dull, shocked understanding I knew what the odd thickness of the frame behind it meant. I knew the meaning of the strange texture of the wood, the fine ridges pressed together dense as the grooves on a record. Thousands upon thousands of sliver-thin frames. Beyond the doorway, sunset filtered through narrow bars of bone-white birch.

The old man turned away from us, cradling the rabbit on his shoulder like a sleeping child. "You are free to leave whenever you please," he said, and stepped out into the light.

Tania Fordwalker lives on an island downunder, as she appreciates the value of a really big moat. Part of the Clarion West '22 cohort, her stories have appeared in *Reactor, Lightspeed, Beneath Ceaseless Skies, Gizmodo, Podcastle,* and more. She has the clicky wrists appropriate to a former Disney animator, strong opinions about airlocks, a tick-borne red meat allergy (worst superpower ever), a pending doctorate, and ADHD, obviously. You can find her work online at www.TaniaWalker.com.

The Government Will Pay For Your Funeral

Offor Chidera

death cheapens over layered petroleum / so
dense, fishes come upon land to un-breathe;
so dense: we the humans, pococurante—yet we
light torches for the final act of purification.

We pull landscapes into our hungry mouths & spit out
Tiny morsels of heaven. My sister burned the national cake,

Becoming the first among us to die in protest. Her spirit hovers
In the pipe network of our bathroom, like a mess of calloused hair,

Waiting for another baptism down a historical drain.

the earth is a drinker of running blood / and
if we live long enough, each drop of blood
will concatenate, liter per liter,
shape-shifting into black gold.

Her skin renders to a dead serenade: unboxing
& unburying each lost soul at organic phases of white sand.

She bone-feeds it firm, against iron, sojourning toward light,
& Then down the abyss, against ragged realities of life as a wheel.

The axle holds a mound of humus, her ash, while I squeeze extra
Angles into her perspective—her pulse, tongue;

Her lips pursed, poignant, relegating to me all that she was—
Even dead; & all she tried to become.

Offor Chidera (t[he]y) is a Nigerian Poet residing in Coal City. They have been published in *The Spectacle, So To Speak* (print), *Reckoning, Ouch! Collective* and elsewhere. Find them on Bluesky: chideraoffor.bsky.social.

The X That Means Both Death and Life

Ariadne Starling

This story begins and ends with the X that means both death and hope.

Three Xs, two strikes, one message: Solidarity.

26 November, 2017.

The Australian government would prefer that we forget this crime against humanity, this X in flesh in the air.

It's a humid, sweaty, overcast day at a protest at Federation Square in the centre of Melbourne. Shen Narayanasamy of the progressive activist group GetUp! tells us that the police are beating with batons the refugee men who have spent 21 days in peaceful protest against their detention on Manus Island, Australia's refugee detention centre in Papua New Guinea. SHAME read the signs in the square. FOUR YEARS TOO LONG. *We're doing this today at the request of the men, to rise to the dignity of their example.* Natasha Blucher of the Asylum Seeker Resource Centre tells us whistleblowers' accounts of the Nauru camp, another offshore Australian refugee detention centre. *Amazing locals put themselves at risk to get us, journalists, food, and water into the camp.* The smell: There was two weeks' worth of garbage that the men had tried to collect and contain. Pulling water from a well with an oily film on top. Ingenious fresh-water catchment, bed sheets tied up with bottles at the bottom. Every cubicle in the toilets was full to the brim with diarrhoea. The men were so sick and had serious illnesses from three or four years locked up. Even in that toxic place, the refugees' culture of hospitality prevailed. *We ate biscuits that somebody had baked in the middle of a siege. They brought tea for us and added sugar. They'd saved it for guests.* HUMAN RIGHTS ABUSE A CRIME spake the signs. STOP VILIFYING REFUGEES. In the crowd I see Hijabi Muslim women of colour, young white guys in shorts, and many seniors holding photos of the refugees who have died in Australian camps. There have been 14 known refugee deaths in offshore detention since 2014, including 7 by suicide. Senior women with purple shirts saying *Grandmothers against children in detention.*

The crowd is asked to kneel, or sit if we can't kneel, for four minutes, with our hands crossed above our heads, which is the way that the men of Manus had been protesting for 21 days. We squat or sit with difficulty for four minutes, hearing the words of Kurdish-Iranian asylum seeker Behrouz Boochani's statement, his dignity, his gratitude for our support. There is the hideous dissonance of a *Wallace & Gromit* exhibition ad in huge letters behind the crowd squatting with their hands crossed. The ad silently blares *It's hard to wipe the smile off your face!* Behrooz's statement is haunting: despite having not enough food themselves, the refugees had been feeding their dogs, and the police had killed one out of spite.

The sun breaks through the clouds and is thanked for it by a grateful speaker. Activists who used to teach at Victoria University speak with admiration of their migrant and refugee students' resourcefulness. The small moments of humour are some of the most striking. Leading us in the squat, a speaker says *It's okay to sit if you can't squat, if your knees aren't, you know, pilates.* The crowd chuckles, and I think about those small moments of levity, not because we're having fun, but because we recognise our shared humanity, our vulnerability.

This X is in flesh in the air, arms crossed in solidarity, the X of the refugee men's arms iconic of their captivity. The X that represents the deaths from which they flee and to which our policies have driven them. But their X is the hope of protest too, of shackles to be broken, and ours a tribute to their dignity and their deep humanity, unassailable.

Australia's federal government would prefer that we forget this crime against humanity, this X in flesh in the air. Will you let them?

13 November, 2019.

This X is the target that Aboriginal people have had on them in this colonised country for over 230 years. It is the X in the scope of a gun, too often turned on Black men, women, and gender-diverse people by police in this colony.

It is a grey day at the snap rally Justice for Kumanjayi Walker, a 19-year-old Warlpiri Aboriginal man who was shot by police in his home in Yuendumu, 300 km north-west of Alice Springs, in central Australia, on Saturday 9 November, 2019. A crowd begins to gather at the intersection of Bourke and Elizabeth Streets. A man with a sad expression, lines on his forehead, and a streak of rich red hair licking up from the right of his forehead addresses a circle of orange-and-yellow high-vis supporters. No microphone, but I see him mouth *They say it'll be a rally in the rain, well it'll rain. Those of you who've done this before* . . . . A fat Black man with a clipped beard and red Indigenous-design dots across a red sports-style vest leans his face into the chest and over the left shoulder of a thin man in front of him, taking comfort from him. Two little Black girls huddle together under their Aboriginal flag to protect them from the beginning rain. A sign rises over the crowd. THE FUTURE IS BLACK. A chill wind blows down Elizabeth St and through the pillars I stand between at the top of the Bourke St post office steps.

The signs are heartbreaking. I see women looking desolate under hand-written and printed signs KILLED IN CUSTODY, the red and yellow letters stark against the black background. A fierce, articulate Black man gestures with his right hand as a bank of cameras point at him, *Terra Nullius is a legal fiction!* (*Terra Nullius*, Latin for "nobody's land," was the legal principle used by British settler-colonists to justify stealing the territory of Australia from its Aboriginal Traditional Owners during British colonisation in the late eighteenth century.) A woman with short white hair nods during the speeches, an Aboriginal flag rises above the lowered zip of her open black hoodie. Her mouth wobbles, she bends her head down to her left hand to wipe a tear, never putting down her sign *End the brutality! Stop the killings! Justice for Wayne!* Her stricken face resonates between the placards and I can't look away from her grief. The sacred smoke of burning eucalyptus leaves rises over the crowd in a wind that blows down Bourke St. An Aboriginal Elder raises his voice and a smooth dark brown staff and projects to us his name and his Country, and that he is from the Stolen Generations. He raises his hands to the sky and describes the spirits he is connected with—*I have been blessed.* A ripped cardboard sign rises before me, BLACK LIVES MATTER with strong strokes in yellow and red. The crowd has swelled and fills the tram tracks. I see the kind eyes of Aunty Tanya Day smiling from a poster.

Jaeden Williams, a Yalukit Willam man of the Boon Wurrung people, speaks. *My family have been here for 4,000 generations, for 100,000 years. This land has a story that is a lot longer than 150 years. According to the Boon Wurrung, this land was created by Bunjil, who travels as an eagle. He taught us to welcome all friends and guests. Bunjil's Laws are two promises, and these promises have been the essence of the land since time began.* He asks the crowd to speak after him, and we join our voices to say,

We promise
to look after the land

and the water
and we promise
to look after the children

That's been the spirit of this land, of Melbourne, of my culture, since time began.

A sign, white text on a black background:

16 . 03 . 2019
Veronica Baxter 34
IDENTIFIED AS A WOMAN
THROWN IN A MALE PRISON
FOUND HANGING IN CELL

Does anyone have clapsticks? asks a speaker. The powerful Elder raises his staff and says, *I've got a weapon of mass destruction!* and the crowd laughs along with him. A woman speaker asks us to put a hand over our hearts—*Breath in from our ancestors*. The crowd is silent, stricken faces, the pulse-pulse of our hands tapping a heartbeat on the cloth over our hearts. After finishing, *I think our ancestors heard us*. A tram leaves the intersection toward Queen St.

A speaker reads statements from Elders in the area, later published in *The Saturday Paper*.

From Marly Wells Naparngardi, a Warlpiri woman: *We came on Sunday morning to stand together in our grief and were presented with smirking police officers and no answers. Two mounted police attempted to bring their horses closer, an intimidation tactic. Someone requested them to leave and I heard one of the officers say, "If you had any respect for the horse's life you would stop waving the cardboard in its face. He doesn't like it. You're intimidating him." If you had any respect for human beings, if you had any respect for the Traditional Owners of this land, if you had any respect at all, you would be questioning the systems in place—the systems you benefit from, the systems that keep Aboriginal people down.* "SHAME!" breaks out and spreads across the crowd.

A person of colour in a white knit jumper and navy headscarf holds a sign spray-painted on the back, beneath three inverted triangles in the queer anarchist movement's pink and black,

QUEERS
AGAINST

COLONIAL
-ISM!

A man sings a Warlpiri song, a sad melody, and translates after every line—*He's missing his kids*. Signs are held over heads as the rain begins. *Police must not investigate police!* A woman with a rainbow beanie asks to take a little boy with pale short hair past me down the steps to see the speakers. The crowd cheers a speaker and the boy turns around in his bright giraffe-print coat to give her the thumbs-up. The boy explains to her that he's giving the thumbs-up to the speakers when the crowd claps to show his support. *Use of bush medicine, cultural practices, and Law*. Between speakers, a quiet descends over the crowd. A baby cries to my left and a motor idles on Elizabeth St.

The wind changes direction and blows up the steps towards me and I smell the sacred smoke of the eucalyptus. The women behind me are trying to find their friends in the crowd. "He's running." "Is he a super fitness nut?" The march begins and I join the back of the crowd and remember the enthusiasm and solidarity. A man and woman's voices begin the chant behind me, *Too many coppers: Not enough justice!* A person with short hair and intricate spiderweb and flower tattoos emerging from their sleeves holds a sign lettered in black, yellow, and red,

TELL
THE
TRUTH

The red of TRUTH drips in the rain down their left wrist off the bottom of the sign, ominous. *Too many coppers!* begins the chant and breaks off into giggles as *Too many coppers!* rolls back from the front of the crowd and confuses the rhythm. We cross Swanston St and bank up, the roar of the crowd swells. A Black woman with short black curls holding her takeaway dinner with a tiny sauce tub on top rests on a short plinth and smiles, and I recognise her expression—gratitude and pride.

19 . 11 . 2004
MULRUNJI 36
DIED IN CELL WITHOUT TREATMENT

Too many cop-pers! Not enough—the crowd breaks off and a

woman in yellow next to me adds hesitantly, *Justice?*

The crowd banks and turns to the left and a woman behind me asks, *Are we stopping here?* and it's because there is a line of police in yellow high-vis in front of the Melbourne East Police Station, the letters of the sign booming towards us in 3D. I realise that the high-vis people I saw at the beginning are there to physically stand between us and the police, to protect us from their potential violence. Our guardians. They wear paper gas masks loose at the side of their necks, just in case, water bottles in their backpacks. The police watch uncomfortably.

We cross Russell St and a woman walking a shopping trolley and carrying a silver walking stick pipes up *No justice, no peace!* as she walks through the intersection. A woman with braids in a short, fluffy, red-lined jumper wheels her wheelchair with the march in front of us. I see two Eureka flags and the Torres Strait Islands flag flicking in the wind of the intersection ahead. A woman with a cane has an Aldi shopping bag and thongs—her feet look cold! She turns and laughs at her friend, a generous smile that rises from her cheeks under ginger bangs and hair trailing her shoulders and spilling out of a knitted beanie. A man with a sign, "Do ya want some water, Schazz?" "Yes please." A silver-haired man in a red beanie and a worn leather jacket with a small gum branch tucked over his ear grins and embraces a friend. I see the two rows of guardians bringing up the rear of our march. Water trickles down the tram tracks. I see the boy with the giraffe-print jacket in fluoro pink gumboots at the edge of the crowd.

The crowd banks up at the Parliament steps.

In 2017, Aunty Tanya Day fell asleep on a train after drinking and was woken up and arrested by police under an archaic law for public drunkenness that has been historically disproportionately used to incarcerate Aboriginal people. During her four hours in a cell, she fell and injured her head, unsupervised. When she was discovered, it took an ambulance one hour to arrive. She never awoke and died in hospital.

At the protest, Tanya's daughter Apryl Watson speaks, her voice struggling from the emotion: *We've seen again and again deaths in custody, straight-up murder.* Her voice is exhausted. *Can you tell me how many people went to the Melbourne Cup, got blind drunk—How many whitefellas died in a cell? How many white women had ambulances? They didn't give a shit about mum.* Her voice breaks down at the end of her line. *I've got my daughter at home, I can't even have her sitting next to me when I get breathalysed, she's crying because she doesn't know what's gonna happen to me, because she knows what happened to mum.*

The sinking sun illuminates the stone-faced pillars and the tiny gold sphere is a dot in the inscrutable sunglassed eyes of every cop on the steps of Parliament.

We hear the righteous anger of a speaker. *12 years ago my nephew was found handcuffed in an alley and do you think anything happened to them police? The look of 'em, looking at us like we're dickheads. They're racists, they're murderers! Every year this is happening! This Victorian government here was the first Constitution—Terra Nullius began here. If we had sovereignty recognised in this country, would we be in their jails? Would they be stealing our children?* His voice rises to a sharp growl. *They don't give a fuck about us!*

A line of Black women at the front hold up red-painted palms to the police line as we in the crowd chant *Blood on your hands!* Apryl Watson, her palms reddened, wipes her face with the back of her hand and, looking exhausted, walks down the steps.

Since her death, Aunty Tanya Day's family fought for the Victorian state public drunkenness law to be abolished, and the law is set to be abolished on Melbourne Cup Day in November 2023.

Constable Zachary Rolfe faced a murder trial for the shooting of Kumanjayi Walker. He was acquitted of all criminal charges by an entirely non-Indigenous jury. It was the first time a Northern Territory police officer was charged with an Aboriginal death in custody since the Royal Commission into Aboriginal Deaths in Custody in 1991. There have been at least 517 Aboriginal deaths in custody since the release of the Commission's report. No Australian police officer has ever been convicted of an Aboriginal death in custody.

9 May, 2018.

This X is the axis along which wages crawl in economic graphs, with productivity and profits soaring upwards together into the corner like a banker's hollow smile. This X means an early death for those who can no longer afford to live in Australia.

Lots of morning coffee is being clutched at the Australian Council of Trade Union's first Change the Rules strike. The sun is bright on Lygon St and the crowd smells of aftershave, perfume, and cigarettes. People hand out socialist newspapers reading "Corporate Greed is Bleeding Australia Dry!" I overhear conversation between guys in hoodies and boots, *They're saying $85 billion in tax cuts.* The union initialisms on every side—NIW AEU NIMF MUA CFMEU—teachers, nurses, midwives, maritime and construction workers and more. The Greens triangle marches around above the crowd on invisible arms. A woman laughs on the way past, *I've got the wrong shoes, the wrong shoes.* I see fierce veteran Boomer activists with grey-streaked hair. The union's Eureka flag in Indigenous colours flicks in the wind among the Australian Services Union (clerical workers). Big white blokes welcome each other with big handshakes. *How are ya, mate? Where you bin workin'?* I hear the growing boom of a helicopter, the first of the day. The socialist red flag flying high atop Trades Hall. An Indigenous man in a knitted beanie wears his nation's flag proudly as a cape. Luke Hilakari, Trades Hall Secretary, tells us that we are 60,000 people strong on the streets of Melbourne. *We do not wanna be a country of the working poor. For so long, big business have been feeding us crumbs, like we're pigeons. We're not pigeons. When the 1% have as much as 70%, the system is broken. Inequality is at a 70-year high. It hasn't been this high since the Great Depression.* Luke booms, *Do you want equal pay for women?* The crowd roars *YES!*

A speaker introduces Mahani, who is here representing 100,000 farm workers with the National Union of Workers. Overwhelmingly casual. No penalty rates. Paid cash-in-hand well below the legal minimum wage. Mahani introduces herself as a migrant farm worker from Malaysia. She has a high woman's voice and a Malaysian accent. She sounds a little shrill through the speakers—who doesn't when they have to pro*ject*?—but her message is clear. *We need work rights! We need better future!* Speaking of undocumented migrant workers' harsh black-market labour conditions, she says, *We need amnesty now!* White blokes who'd roared their support for Luke now stand around scoffing and laughing, wincing at her voice through the speakers. These moments don't make it into the press coverage, but they're some of the most important to remember. I am reminded that solidarity is not a status we achieve, but a horizon we work towards, and that our movements regularly fail people of colour. Mahani, migrant woman of colour, activist and union leader, braves our crowd's bullshit and our country's hostility to stand up to speak for 100,000 farm workers being exploited all over Australia.

A speaker booms, *What does the government think when they think that they can turn around and tell youse who you can elect as union leaders? I say to all of you, people from all unions, when they came after them, they come for all of us!* Sally McManus, Secretary of the Australian Council of Trade Unions, the peak trade union body, tells the crowd that 40% of Australian workers are in insecure work. 732 corporations paid not one cent of tax. 62 people who earned more than $1 million in a year paid not one cent of tax, not even the Medicare levy. Guys giggle about the difficulty of holding signs in the wind. *Nah I'm good holding the flag here, might swap when I need a cigarette. Won't have one yet though, might burn the flag!* A tune starts up from a brassy marching band behind us. I first heard the tune as a kid in country Queensland, knowing it by the earlier folk song lyrics, *John Brown's body lies a-mouldering in the grave* overlaid with the union movement's 1915 lyrics to become their rallying song, "Solidarity Forever." But I still hear *John Brown's body* in the melody, and it only makes the union's version more urgent—the failure of the union is a body in the grave.

The National Tertiary Education Union, my crew, in purple shirts and whistles. *Education Not Exploitation! Casuals Against Casualisation!* There are lots of young women among us. *Postgrads and casuals on strike! No more unpaid work!* Pink-scarfed, purple-haired, chatty, checking phones. Someone starts up a snare drum. A woman unionist tells us that the stereotype of a unionist is a man with a hard hat, but in Australia but the average unionist is a woman with a degree. Among the union's contingent at a later rally, I hear Nic Kimberly, a casual academic, address the crowd. The Australian Catholic University threatened Nic with revoking his PhD scholarship for criticising casualisation in progressive national newspaper *The Age*. His voice gets stronger and more defiant as he says, *So what did I do to respond? I became the union branch President!* In the crowd, the conversation continues around me. *It's not about someone coming to uni to have that transformative experience anymore. It's about getting bums on seats, and not long while we're making money.* Elsewhere, I hear, *we've got a problem with homeless students.* A silver-haired union woman waves to kids in the windows on Lygon St. The chilly winds of late Autumn blow down Victoria St as we walk through the intersection. Bystanders bop to the brass band as we slowly march. *A first degree shouldn't cost a mortgage!* Onlookers grin, take phone videos. Flyers, flags and protesters have filled the street as far as the eye can see from Swanston to Queen St. A woman of colour wears leopard-print, sunnies and huge heart earrings with *Militant* in curvy script inside. The other side, I later see, reads *Feminist*. A flag flicks across the back of my neck, a surprising intimacy. A red-and-black jester-clothed trumpet player is cheered by the crowd. A sign says *I'm young and insecure and so is my work!* There is a crisp wind from behind and welcome pockets of sunshine and the slow spin of autumn leaves lifted on winds between skyscrapers. Smiling women in office windows wave invisible flags with us in solidarity. Photographers perch on every tram stop and plinth along our way to capture our march's glorious sprawl.

Flyers paper the fancy cars parked in the middle of Bourke St. A kid in blue gumboots and a Superman shirt is wheeled through the march—despite chants, clappers, trumpets, and drums—completely asleep.

We pick up marchers, chants and energy as we make our way down Swanston St. A guy faceplants on the tram island and is helped by everyone. *You right, brother?* A voice reads out a news update behind me, *City streets shut down as 50,000 march.* A grumpy skinny corporate guy in a tight blue suit cuts through the crowd at an intersection. A speaker says, *It's about the young people we work with every day. They are ripped off in their jobs. They're forced to jump through hoops to access inadequate Newstart* (the unemployment welfare payment). *We don't want them to become the working poor of the future.* Troy Carter tells the crowd about the Esso (ExxonMobil) workers: *Sacked, then offered their jobs back at up to 40% less.* It would be 742 days before the strike ended in a deal. Troy speaks about the effect on his family, on his children being bullied at school. *My children have forced themselves into a shell to avoid being rejected. When I stood outside UGL* (the contractor for Esso)*, their Payroll Officer yelled, "How's your kids, Troy?" and laughed.* Colin Long speaks, Secretary of the Victorian National Tertiary Education Union: *50% of undergraduate teaching is performed by casuals, many working casually for 5, 10, 15 years. Low super, no leave. It should be a scandal that one of our members found herself unable to leave an abusive relationship because of being totally financially dependent. Our researchers find cures for cancer, we develop renewable energy.* We write to chart the course of the history we are living. *Are you ready to change the rules?* The farm workers' signs, stark and true: NO PICKERS NO FOOD NO FUTURE.

This X means early death for the workers whose wages have flatlined along the X axes of economics graphs. But while the union movement lives there is always hope for a better future.

15 March, 2019.

It's a clear day, sunshine, with a cool breeze outside the Old Treasury Building on Spring St as the crowd gathers for the global School Strike 4 Climate. An old woman with a walker, moving slowly, sunnies and a straw hat, makes her way through the intersection, a sign on her walker saying *1.5 to stay alive, stop climate change!* Indigenous men in white paint clack clapsticks from atop a plinth, gum branches held to their comrades. A teenage girl's voice rises above the crowd. *My name's Gaia, I'm a 17-year-old school striker and I'm here because I want a future on this planet. We acknowledge that we meet on the stolen lands of the Boon Wurrung people and there is no climate justice without First Nations justice.* The men raise their arms from the plinth and roar their strength. Two choppers hover over the intersection. *Striking for our future*, says a sign covered in sparkly writing and kids' drawings. *Stop giving us an excuse to skip school!* The speaker continues, *Make some noise if this is your first protest!* I hear a roar reaching down the hill past Treasury Gardens that warms my heart. Grey-haired activists look on and smile. The sign pun/meme game at this protest is exquisite. My friends see me writing down slogans and make sure that I've noted the choicest quotes: *There was one earlier, a picture of Tony Abbott* (the ultra-conservative former Prime Minister filmed eating a raw onion like an apple), *said "No onions on a dead planet." Kids wouldn't have to act like politicians if politicians didn't act like kids! Prime Minister has a pet rock—He's so coal.* A handful of girls and a woman appear on the balcony of the Old Treasury building before being shooed off. A young woman's voice across the crowd: *20,000 people are here, 20,000!* and we roar. An Indigenous speaker says: *We need to listen to my Country, to the Law of my ancestors.* A sign says, *I came here because I hate Melbourne weather. Climate change is not an elective!* I hear, *There's a drone!* and I see it, tiny creature hovering smoothly with its black legs. *Grumpy old man who supports students. Don't frack the future* alongside the Midwives' Union. *Teachers for Climate Justice.* A speaker says that 100 companies cause 71% of climate change. An Aboriginal woman is walking with her kids, something written in the elegant rhythms of an Indigenous language over an illustration of the Aboriginal flag and the earth. A translation on the back of the sign says *Little faces, powerful hearts, we stand together.* I ask her, *What language is that?* She replies *Gunnai!* with pride. *It's beautiful.* My queer community are here: *Gay for Renewables!*

We listen to the urgent speeches of teenage girls in the microphone, *Everyone who's an activist and also a student, get everyone at your school*, the crowd cheers, whistles and kazoos trumpet from all around. *Keep the Earth clean, it's not Uranus.* I see the rainbow sheen of fresh-blown bubbles rising from the corner near the Treasury Gardens and floating away. We cluster in the shade of the buildings at the edge of the crowd. A baby in a sling on her mum's front is holding a cardboard sign saying *Nap strike for climate.* Kids are front and centre on the steps of Old Treasury. The crowd is happy, energetic, diverse, loud, and dynamic. *Climate change is union business* on the black shirt of a charismatic fat lady with red lipstick who's walking a little girl by the hand. *Coal: Drop it coz it's HOT.* Marchers have brought a massive rainbow flag, silky and tall as two people. I notice later that it says WE ARE UNION. *Proud teacher! Scared human.* Kids' fresh chalk drawings fade between the tram lines on the street, trees and earth in pinks and greens. Kids in school uniforms sit on the curb, grinning into their milkshakes. *I'd rather be at school than telling you to do your job.* A sign says *My kids are revolting—proud dad.* Tourists and businesspeople and shoppers look on happily from the street. I love the way the kids' use of pop culture fuels their activism. *Every disaster movie starts with scientists being ignored.*

The crowd has poured into Treasury Gardens, and there are dogs barking, picnics, kids cheering, a speaker announcing solidarity with the Standing Rock Sioux water protectors. White women in yellow high-vis security vests, *Where's the baaand, Jenny, I thought you said there was gonna be a band?!* A speaker passionately exclaims, *We are not your enemy! Farming communities are not your enemy! We are the ones being hit worst by climate change.* A woman's voice in the mic: *I'm glad to know I'm not the only one who goes home every night who thinks, what is going to happen to my kids when I'm dead and gone?* A speaker says *My dad is a farmer. His dad is a farmer. I wanted to be a farmer but there won't be anything left to FARM.* The police estimate 50,000 people in Melbourne alone.

Attending the Melbourne protest of Donald Trump's inauguration on 21 January 2017, a friend asks me, *What's the point?* I say, *We have to do something, we have to let them know that this is not okay.* Critiquing the dismissal of activist events as "preaching to the choir," Rebecca Solnit writes:

> [Researcher Erica Chenoweth] concluded that only around 3.5 percent of a population was needed to successfully resist or even topple a regime non-violently. In other words, to create change, you don't need everyone to agree with you; you just need some people to agree so passionately that they will donate, campaign, march, risk arrest or injury, possibly prison or death. Their passionate conviction may influence others. Ideas originate at the margins and migrate inwards to succeed; insisting that your idea must have arrived rather than be traveling is to miss how change works.

This X is the death of all life, what awaits us if we do nothing, if we don't do enough, the X for extinction in the centre of Extinction Rebellion's hourglass logo. But this X also means hope. Our hope lies in the fight not yet over, in the leadership of young people and Elders who show us the way. The hourglass is not finished, but time is running out.

This story begins and ends with the X that means both death and hope.

Three Xs, two strikes, one message: Solidarity forever.

"The X That Means Both Death and Life" originally appeared in Unlikely Stories *in July 2023.*

Dr. Ariadne Starling is an award-winning writer from Melbourne working in literary essays, sex writing, and queer literature. Her work explores sexuality, disability, neurodiversity, culture, identity, and social justice. She has won 5 national and international scholarships and 16 awards for academic and creative writing—starting at the age of 11. She was shortlisted for the Overland Fair Australia Essay Prize and the City of Melbourne Lord Mayor's Creative Writing Award for Narrative Nonfiction. She has published in *Transcultural Studies*, *Colloquy*, *Cordite Poetry Review*, and *Verity La*.

Fixing the System in Tilt Town

Kat Murray

When I was little, my parents died trying to reach Lady Luck. My brother Maynard says the journey was hard back then. These days, it's easier for people to worship at her feet.

What she demands as sacrifice isn't so straightforward.

"There's *nothing* for him in this town." Maynard's voice is bitter as he watches Clay skip off to school on his ninth birthday. My nephew is a sweet boy, all shining hazel eyes under a thatch of curly dark hair that reminds us of his late mother. She died when Lady Luck frowned on her, but nobody mentions that. It's just one of those things.

A few days ago, I tried to show Clay how I wanted to streamline the house's microfiltration system, but Maynard told me to cut that shit out. Clay is destined for greater things. In two months, the boy will enter the education lottery and then he might be able to get out of here.

"It's not fair," Maynard continues. "Getting that bitch Luck to smile ain't easy for people like me. Not these days."

My brother lapses into a stony silence. I'm loath to break it. I turn my eyes without moving my head, checking on Gran. She's blessedly asleep.

Maynard picks up one of my stray models I meant to put away. Wires twist intricately through a pair of oversized buttons, each one representing airflow—the beginnings of an idea I have, if I ever get to design it. Maynard's broad thumb crushes the delicate thing. Wires bend beyond recognition as he continues to ruminate.

"Clay needs an extra boost," he declares. "Something to get him through that lottery and into the City, where he'll have more chances."

Under the table where my brother can't see, I let my hands and toes fidget. "A visit to Lady Luck?" I whisper.

"Damn straight." Maynard bares yellowed teeth in a kind of smile. "We'll leave in three days."

We?

Maynard reveals more of his teeth as he preempts my next

question. "You're coming with me, Cassie. Gran, too."

"What about Clay?" I ask.

"He'll stay in town. It isn't a problem finding someone to look after *him* for a month."

Once my brother makes a decision, nothing sways him. Fear of the unknown rivets me to the hard plastic chair. But a shiver of excitement lurks underneath.

I've always wanted to leave town. There's nothing for me here, either.

The hours tick down to our departure. I can't shake my unease. I've mapped out our journey a dozen times, tracing the way past other towns all the way to the ocean. Lady Luck lives at the edge of the water, near enough the City to constantly watch over its unmoving houses, high walls, and thick gates.

To get to her, we'll have to pass perilously near Tilt Town.

Tilter streets are crooked gashes across steep hills, nothing like the neat layout of normal towns. Instead of balancing on treads and wheels, their dwellings cling to the soil any which way they can, because the earth often shifts underneath Tilt Town.

That's how the place got its name. The inhabitants must constantly be ready to readjust the slant of their living quarters, to recut stilts and shore up bedrooms and kitchens so they can sleep and eat without rolling sideways.

Maynard says the Tilters don't worship Lady Luck hard enough, even though they practically live at her feet, and that's why none of them are successful. When I misbehaved as a kid—which was often—he'd threaten to send me there. Now, even though I'm long past the days of overt meltdowns, the thought of Tilt Town makes me shiver.

Across the room, near the driver's capsule, Gran moans from her recliner. I'm glad for an excuse to fold the map. The house sways slightly on its treads as I fetch a precious measure of water. Maynard says it doesn't matter at this point if Gran ingests microplastics, so he forbade me to use the house's inbuilt filtering system for her. Instead, I take out one of my homemade contraptions, decanting a small amount into Gran's favorite cup. Her lips press against worn enamel. She can barely manage to drink by herself these days.

I wish Gran and I could stay behind with Clay, but Maynard is right. Nobody here would take us in.

I hold Gran's bony hand and explain our upcoming journey. With her, I always presume competence. I taught Clay to do the same, even though Gran is mostly listless, gazing out the window into our yard, where we manage to cultivate a crop of hardy vegetables.

But when I tell Gran we're going to see Lady Luck to help Clay get out of here, her filmy blue eyes clear and harden.

"No, Cassie," she tells me. "No."

Maynard is dismissive of Gran's reaction. "She loved Clay and wanted the best for him," he snaps. "We're leaving tomorrow, come hell or high water."

I don't push, because now that Clay is old enough to be more independent, Maynard gets stressed out by me still living with him. Gran and I, we're *a lot*. That's what he says when he's fed up.

Maynard is a pillar of the community, a deputy police chief, so his word carries weight around here. But that isn't enough to guarantee Clay a spot in the City.

Lady Luck must smile on my nephew for that.

In the living room, all my magazines are stacked in order. My precious parts are laid out in perfect lines, ready to be packed for our journey. A graphite filter sits next to a hunk of solar panel I salvaged from the town dump. I have screws, wires, nets, bits of metal, and a box of tools. I make sure to pack everything safely away before Maynard comes in. He hates it when I mess around trying to invent stuff, because then I have less time to clean and look after Gran.

But later, after I've read Clay a bedtime story and tucked him in, Maynard pulls me aside. "Do one more check of the house, Cassie. Make sure the engine and treads are good so we're ready to roll tomorrow."

I can't help but smile. He wouldn't have asked if he didn't trust my mechanical know-how. Maybe Lady Luck will smile upon me, too.

The morning of our departure dawns hot and bright, a reminder that fire season starts soon. Five years ago, everyone had to drive their houses to the town's auxiliary parking lot and hunker down to avoid a nearby blaze. That's the furthest I've ever traveled.

Until today.

I make a bet with Clay, wagering that he'll grow at least half a centimeter while we're gone. If he doesn't, he'll give me his best marble. If he does, I'll craft him a new toy.

He asks for an airplane, lips turning up in that amazing little smile of his. We rush to measure him against the doorframe once more, and then he heads to school, waving three times at the gate—once for each extra hug I gave him this morning.

I watch him until he's out of sight.

Maynard makes me pick the vegetables from our garden, even though it's too early. Half of them are severely underripe, but he says better us getting them than someone else. Then Maynard starts up the house's engine and we roll out toward the town's front gate.

I hang out a side window, a kind of freedom blowing through my hair. Even before Gran needed fulltime care, I didn't get out and about much. I was always the weird girl, the annoyance at the edges who broke the social rules over and over until it was better for me to stay out of sight, out of mind.

Sometimes it feels like I'm not really part of the community anymore, but maybe that's unavoidable in a town where people prize individualism above all.

Old Ulrich who guards the gates gives me a look I'm used to, somewhere between pity and contempt. His gaze flickers over Gran in her recliner. I watch uneasily as Ulrich's lips twist.

"May it be enough." Ulrich nods at Maynard and turns his gaze toward the distance again, watching for interlopers who might try to infiltrate the town, or steal our vegetables, or whatever interlopers do.

The gate shuts behind us, and we're truly on our way.

We drive west, watched with suspicion by the Ulrich-equivalents at each semi-identical town gate. On day four, we stop to repair one of the house's treads. Then our sewage filtration system breaks down, but with a little fiddling, I rig up a fix that'll hold us for the journey.

After two weeks of travel, the towns dwindle until we are surrounded by sere hills whose tan flanks guide us downward until we spot the ocean in the distance. I have never seen so much water in one place, except in pictures. But although the silvery-blue streak on the horizon is alluring, my eyes are drawn toward the jagged skyline of Tilt Town. At night, the town glows with a hellish flame from the pit on its outskirts, the depths burning endlessly. At school, we learned that's because of an unholy combination of natural gasses and whatever the Tilters throw down there. My classmate Paisley said they threw in babies, and the teacher didn't correct her.

"Aren't you happy I didn't ship your ass to the Tilters when you used to have all those tantrums over stupid crap like food textures and the wrong socks?" Maynard gestures to the wheel. "Take a shift. I need to stretch my legs."

As I sit, Maynard slams the reinforced door behind him. Because of his job, he got extra security features for his house, so the driver's capsule is wholly secure, like a commercial airplane's cockpit of old. Or a panic room.

Later that afternoon, I feed Gran from her favorite cup, but she turns her head at every spoonful. My worry turns into fear. She's growing weaker.

"Look," I whisper. "We're nearly to the ocean. In a few hours, we'll see Lady Luck."

Gran raises one bony hand in a weak signal, index finger extended. Maybe she's trying to sign Go, but her hand splays, and falls, and it turns into more of a No.

We arrive near sunset. Lady Luck towers above us, easily ten times as tall as Maynard. She stands knee-deep in ocean water, the tide lapping at her pearlescent marble skirts. One hand is upraised, as if to offer consecration. The other holds the leash of a giant stone dog, green-hued and brindled with salt. Lady Luck's thin lips press together, neither smiling nor frowning.

Yet.

I take a few careful steps onto the beach, searching the tideline for washed-up sacrifice. Maynard crunches past, leaving hard, deep footprints in the sand. He has a recent photograph of Clay, the one in which he's grinning so hard we can see two lost teeth. Maynard stops at the water's edge.

"See the dog?" he asks. "He and Luck always go hand in hand.

He's called Hard Work. Kind of like you."

He laughs. I don't. I have a bad feeling in my stomach, and it isn't because I've been trying to eat the unripe vegetables from our garden.

"Maynard, what are you going to sacrifice?"

My brother kicks off his boots, rolls up his trousers, wades into the water. I want to do the same, to feel the luxury of liquid lapping around my toes, but I'm afraid of Maynard's stance, and especially of the vicious buck knife he's produced.

But I still trust him, don't I?

"Go inside, Cassie. Get Gran ready to move."

Habit makes me obey immediately. But halfway up the beach, I turn for a second look.

Maynard was the one who convinced Clay's mother to keep the baby inside her until full-term, even though pregnancy was killing her. It was a necessary sacrifice, Maynard said. Lady Luck smiled on Clay and took his mother in exchange. But surely Maynard doesn't mean to offer *himself* to the statue.

I pick up my pace. I rush indoors to shift Gran into her wheeled mobility chair. But she kicks, rocking perilously side to side, and I'm afraid she'll fall over—so I wedge her into the driver's capsule between the heavy door and the wall, where she's safest.

Then I crack open the window and watch Maynard wade up to Lady Luck, to the tiny altar of her skirt.

"Here, have it all!" he shouts, and with movements I don't understand, he cuts the air nearby with a knife. A multi-colored aura hovers around the outline of his body, as if hesitating to leave.

"Take my dreams!" Maynard demands. "Take my ambitions!"

The aura coalesces and streams toward Lady Luck—a wonder of a moment, even if it isn't mine to experience. It reaches her marble in a riot of color and settles effervescently into her skirt folds before glowing upward.

When the light reaches her face, Maynard holds up the photo of Clay, and Lady Luck's stern lips lift into a smile focused at the boy.

I should be happy. This could be enough extra luck for Clay to get into the City. But I think, maybe once your own ambitions are all tied up in other folks, the only thing left to do is enforce them.

And Maynard doesn't look satisfied.

Sound carries near water, so I hear Maynard mutter, "Forgive me for what I'm about to do."

I realize, with a cold bolt of certainty, why the townsfolk

averted their gazes as we rolled out of town. Why Ulrich pitied me at the gates. Maynard won't stop at giving up his own dreams and ambitions.

He'll sacrifice me and Gran, too.

I slam the capsule door shut. Jam my foot onto the pedal. We move at a crawl at first, but it's enough to soothe Gran's restlessness. She signs *go. Go. Go.*

Maynard's after us, sprinting up the beach, sunset glinting orange off his drawn knife.

I activate the fireproof panels. They creep slowly downward, shooting the house's fuel economy to hell. But we're already in hell, so what does it matter?

The weight of Maynard's body hitting the porch makes the house bounce on its treads. A warning light flashes on the dashboard as one of the panels halts.

My brother wrenches open the unlocked back door with a colossal bang.

He's already bellowing threats, storming his way to the driving area, fists bashing against metal. He's thwarted, furious, dangerous. A kind of fury stirs within me, too, something I haven't been allowed for years. I want the best for Clay. But not at the expense of my own dreams—or Gran's life.

I steer us uphill. Toward Tilt Town.

"Cassie!" Maynard bawls. "Come out right now!"

Defiance, long dormant, makes me crank the house's speed to maximum. At the door, Maynard's fists go ominously quiet. Footsteps creak down the hallway. They return faster than I'd like.

"Cassie," Maynard says more quietly. "I have an axe. Open up *now,* or you'll get hurt."

When I was Clay's age, Gran tried to teach me how to tell the difference between bluffing and truth.

"It's not safe to assume everyone means well," Gran said back when she could string sentences together coherently. "You're a vulnerable type, Cassie. You need to be able to sniff out a lie."

"Lies don't smell," I'd told her, and she'd looked up to the ceiling in despair. Then I'd gone back to my books and my inventions, neither of which are in the habit of being sneaky or untruthful.

Still, I didn't turn out completely naïve.

When I open the capsule door to Maynard, I'm armed with the flare gun he keeps underneath the driver's seat. Like a lot of things, it's a relic of a bygone time. But it'll scorch his face off if I shoot him at close range. Especially since he lied about the axe. He's only got a hatchet.

"You're not sacrificing Gran," I tell him. "Or me."

My brother scowls, but he backs away, moving to the side to let us pass as we reach the living room. I keep the gun pointed at his face as I bend to grab my box of personal possessions. I take a photo of Clay, too. Maynard sneers as I stow my stuff in the compartment underneath Gran's mobility chair.

"Your inventions and books won't keep you alive," my brother says. "Not in Tilt Town."

Maybe he's right. But there are worse fates.

I wheel Gran backward with one hand. Thump her over the threshold, past the slender lines of ink that show Clay's growth over the years. My throat is tight but my eyes are dry. I keep the flare gun pointed, even when the house begins to move again.

Maynard drives away, abandoning us at the side of the road as night descends.

I wheel Gran upward. There's nowhere else to go, so we head in the direction of Tilt Town.

This terrifies me, but if I was wrong about my brother, what else could I have been wrong about? Old aspirations stir at the edges of my mind like long-forgotten fever dreams. Maybe I could get a job, a *real* one—not just cleaning and looking after Clay and Gran.

I used to read job advertisements in the magazines that found their way to us. I'd narrow them down to what a town's education qualified me for. I wanted to be a research assistant. Anything above that required me to have been lucky enough for a college education. But Maynard told me I shouldn't apply. People like me talk wrong, act wrong, think wrong. I'd never fit in, so why bother?

The road is steep, and the night is moonless. Far behind, Lady Luck still glimmers with Maynard's sacrificed dreams. In the hills ahead, the pit casts its orange smolder against distant rooftops. The wheels on Gran's chair squeak until I have to hum under my breath to balance out the painful sound. There's no Maynard to scold me for making annoying noises.

But soon, I'm exhausted and dizzy, and Gran is moaning.

I push us onto the road's shoulder and lift Gran from her chair, making sure her head doesn't droop forward and block off her windpipe. We sink to the ground and I cradle her to me. She is so weak. Even when I explain what's going on, she only twirls my hair gently, in a movement that's somehow both a baby's questing hand and a mother's soothing touch.

There's no point fearing the unknown when death is already in my lap. The chill of the night keeps me from sleeping soundly, but I drop into an occasional doze.

When dawn breaks and I shudder awake for the final time, Gran is dead in my arms, and there's a group of Tilters staring down at us.

Grief numbs my fear. I cannot speak. All I can do is hold Gran's cooling hand.

The Tilters don't look like devils or rapists, like Maynard used to call them. They wear homespun clothes and concerned expressions, and when they help lift Gran's body into her chair, they're gentle. We walk slowly into Tilt Town. I keep hold of Gran's hand, half-expecting it to rise to sign for water, or food, or warmth. It stays still, no matter how I cling.

I'm homeless. No more Gran, no more Clay. I have to recalibrate. But how?

Tilt Town's steep streets and stationary dwellings prove less threatening than I expect. People eye me curiously from doorsteps, but don't ask prying questions. There's no Ulrich equivalent to interrogate me, because there are no gates here.

I still can't talk, so eventually, people call on someone named Big Joan.

"Come on," Big Joan says, brooking no argument. She grasps Gran's chair with hands twice the size of mine, and I follow her broad shoulders toward her residence: a trio of shipping containers loosely welded together. A ramp leads to her living room. Poorly-made pipes run the length of the room, connecting to the bathroom at the far end.

Big Joan pours me half a cup of water through an extremely inefficient filter.

"We get all sorts here, but most of them aren't dead on arrival," the woman tells me in a gruff contralto. "I know you're in shock, but we gotta find a resting place for your loved one. Usually, folks opt to be recycled. Helps crops. Helps others live. Now and then, we get those who wanna be burned or put to the ocean. So, you decide which she would have wanted while I leave you be for a bit."

Big Joan exits the room. While I think about Gran's next steps, I reach for the filter. I have to keep my fingers busy. When I was a kid, I used to break things apart one bit at a time, until Gran gave me tools of my own. Then I turned destroying into fixing.

Tears blur my eyes as I lean past Gran to fetch my box of stuff. I need a focus, or I'll drown in grief. I mend the handle of the portable filter and shore up the gaping left side, where microplastics could leak through. By the time Big Joan returns, I'm wedged under her sink, checking out the house's rudimentary filtration system, which has major problems.

My fingers explore. My brain calms. Big Joan waits.

"Gran would want to be recycled," I say when I recover the ability to speak. "She always tried to teach us to help others."

"What's your name?" Big Joan asks on the second day.

We sit in front of her living room container, our feet propped in the street. Tilters pass by, and each one nods to us. They don't keep themselves to themselves here.

I lift my eyes. The town's arable land lies in the mid distance. Gran's body will contribute to the crops grown there. I remain silent for a few beats, considering Big Joan's question. I don't feel like who I used to be.

"Cass," I finally say.

An hour ago, I finished my repairs on Big Joan's house, and now there is no more risk of cross-contamination when the house recycles waste. Previously, she'd had been at high risk of dysentery or cholera. Her filtration system still isn't perfect, but it's much safer.

Fixing it kept me busy, but dread settles across my shoulders, weighing me down until I'm surprised the chair I'm perched on doesn't snap into hundreds of plastic shards. Big Joan told me she often takes in newcomers for a day or two, just until they get on their feet. Now it's time for her to thank me for my work and send me on my way. To where, I don't know. I'm too numb to panic. Probably, I'll find a spot nearby and wait to join Gran. Maynard was right. I have no clue how to live independently.

Then Big Joan speaks, and the chair doesn't break, and everything in me is suddenly light.

"You're good at fixing things, and I'm not. I'd like you to stay with me, Cass," she says. "For as long as you want."

Living with Big Joan gives me the luxury of my own time and space. The Tilters quickly get into the habit of bringing me City trash, which I occasionally turn into useful treasure.

Water is scarce, but the situation is worse here, because the shortage is exacerbated by position. Any rain the Tilters gets runs swiftly down to the City. I wander between propped-up dwellings and make notes on gradients and groundwater and revel in the fact that people here don't interrupt my focus by demanding to know what I'm doing, is the house clean, and what's for supper?

People here constantly rebuild, rejig, reshuffle. In the first month, the ground tilts three times. The movement is somehow both subtle and sudden. One moment, everything is normal. Then, without even seeming to move, the hill slants an extra quarter of a centimeter away from the City—as if the place is weighing down the world, making Tilt Town rise to precarious heights. The pit shifts ever-closer, throwing its light over everything.

At night, from the new balcony I welded to Big Joan's upper level, I often stare in Lady Luck's direction. When she glows from recent sacrifice, she lights distant pale walls, lending the City an extra moon's worth of gentle whiteness. At times like that, her shadow falls across Tilt Town, dampening the constant orange glow of the pit. It's an uneasy darkness, layered like a series of bloodstains seen only under UV light.

Seasons pass. I wouldn't bother to count them if it weren't for Clay.

By now, he's twelve. When one of the Tilters manages to acquire premium internet, we crowd around a screen and carve up the time into precious minutes. One day, my curiosity becomes too much, and I make myself join in. My fingers fly over the keyboard. Clay's name pops up almost immediately.

Maynard's sacrifice was enough. Lady Luck got Clay a spot at a moderately prestigious City school. I move away from the screen, wracked with relief, with guilt, even with jealousy—but above all, I just miss my nephew.

He would have grown that half a centimeter by now. In my spare time, I craft him the airplane I'd promised. Not a flimsy toy, but a display model fit for the teenager he'll soon become. Maynard always wanted him to like fighter jets or bombers, but Clay's most treasured models were of commercial airplanes. When I finish, I carve the name of his favorite airline and flight number—one of the last ever flown—into the metal.

Then I wrap it carefully and Big Joan arranges for it to be delivered to his school in the City.

"Do you think he'll like it?" I ask her.

"No point wondering," she says from the kitchen, where she's fixing up a batch of soup for a communal lunch. "You did as much as you have control over."

Big Joan has people skills but not a ton of book smarts, and I'm basically the opposite. What we have, I tell her, is a symbiotic relationship, and she always makes sure to acknowledge observations like that with a serious nod before asking me if I've remembered to stay hydrated. I'm glad for her skills as I help carry bowls and utensils.

Today, we watch the news. Towns like my old one have begun developing slants of their own. There's lots of talk about how to brace treads and build stronger gates.

It's not a disaster yet, the talking heads claim. With enough sacrifice, Lady Luck will smile upon their own. Look at the City, they say. It's slowly sinking, but they're coping.

We'll cope too, right?

Except we don't.

Even my newest inventions cannot get Tilt Town enough water. It hasn't rained more than a few drops for months. We're all going thirsty and unwashed. I've done everything possible: maximized the efficiency of each wastewater system, rigged up extra nets to collect fog and dew, and set my solar desalinization stations to work overtime processing oceanwater.

We don't have enough resources to collect our most-needed resource.

What hurts the most is the way people look at me as if *I* can fix this. In despair one night, I climb to the top of Big Joan's roof with my telescope. Colonizing Mars is a ship that's long since sailed, but watching stars reminds me that the universe is composed of more than just us and the City.

After a long time peering through a homemade telescope, I make out lights that aren't stars. I frown, adjust lenses, and continue observation. The lights turn out to be small, state-of-the-art drones. They circle far above, a glittering, fine mesh stretching between them.

No wonder we're not getting any water. The City is stealing our rain before it even reaches us.

We'll all die if we don't figure out how to change this.

Big Joan calls a meeting. Everyone in Tilt Town comes.

There's an energy that flows in most humans, one that seems to be several parts sectarianism mixed with a large dash of magical thinking and a varying dose of self-preservation. When I announce that we've reached a tipping point, I expect resource-hoarding to commence and for me to be considered a burden again.

But nobody here is overly interested in maintaining the status quo.

So when I'm done explaining, everyone stays quiet. Even stranger, they look to me for a plan.

"I've thought a lot about seesaws," I tell everyone haltingly, encouraged by the way Big Joan stands at my shoulder. "They're logical, but they also taught me about human nature. When you're light, and a heavy kid climbs onto the other side, they might fling you toward the stratosphere. That's what the City's doing. Maybe they don't set out to do it, but it's happening anyway."

"Then what do we do?" a person shouts from the crowd, which has swollen to a size I never expected. We've gotten more town refugees lately.

"What *can* we do?" someone else mutters. "They can steal anything they like and call it their due."

Big Joan steps forward before things get frayed. She thumps a fist against her heart.

"Everyone's got something in them that helps a community. But they aren't always given a chance to show it."

People nod and shuffle at her words. This buys me time to talk about my calculations of force and mass. I arm the crowd with hard numbers, and then I tell them, flat out, the only thing that'll fix this situation.

"It's time to kill Lady Luck."

We march toward the ocean, carrying what we need to topple the phenomenon that killed my parents and saved my nephew. I think of Clay a lot these days. I'm not one for magical thinking, but I choose to believe he got the airplane I sent. That he knows I'm still alive. That I love him.

Lady Luck stands thigh-deep in the water when we arrive, her skirts red with recent sacrifice. As a final act of self-preservation, she smiles upon me, and whispers into my mind that the City wants me, has *always* wanted me, I'm so smart, I'm so *incredibly* useful—but I'm done with Lady Luck's foibles.

I gesture, and the Tilters come forward.

We haul Lady Luck off her pedestal, and the tenuous link between the statue and her dog breaks forever. The canine representation of Hard Work stands alone in the swelling tide as we drag Lady Luck up the steep hill, toward the glowing pit beyond. We're sending her to hell.

By the time we reach the halfway point, we're sweating and trembling with exertion. Lady Luck tries to work her magic on the hundreds of Tilters at her ropes. *It could be you*, she whispers in increasing desperation.

"Statistically improbable!" I take to shouting. A few take up the words, like a rallying cry. Others snap back with their own rejoinders.

"It's *never* people like me," my neighbor bellows, thumping marble with a walking aid.

"It should be all of us!" another person yells.

"No more sacrifice!" Big Joan puts her back into pulling.

The pit's foul miasma hits us, and our breaths turn shallow. The fires below are fueled by City garbage and natural gasses, not Tilter babies like my classmate once claimed. We heave once more. Marble flashes.

A deep groan shudders through the earth as Lady Luck falls headfirst into orange flames.

Lady Luck is dead, and everything changes.

The land underneath Tilt Town begins to sink, levelling out with the City. Because the Tilters are so used to working as a community, we're quick to save our dwellings. Big Joan rushes from place to place, only pausing when we see what's happening to the walls over which Luck once smiled.

They shift, slowly but surely. The City's foundations were never built on level ground to begin with, so its walls sag quickly to one side. People put their hands atop shoulders of children, pointing, saying: *you may never see this again in your lifetime.*

I know this is right, and I also know this is wrong. Like a seesaw unweighted, the earth underfoot continues to settle, and my thoughts turn to Clay. My sweet nephew with his quick smile. If I hadn't had his growth to cherish alongside Gran's slow deterioration and Maynard's hard words, how would I have managed to keep my own balance for so long?

One Tilter sets up a projector and begins streaming footage. For the City, the world has flipped sideways. Walls are floors and floors are walls, and the gates stand wide open to the outside for the first time in centuries. I clench my hands into fists as I watch people run for their lives. I lean in close to the screen. Searching. Hoping. A drone camera zooms in on a group of students rushing toward the gates. They're nearly there when a chunk of masonry smashes into their midst. The frontrunners are unscathed, but one of their fellows is trapped, legs waving, screaming for help. My stomach twists.

A sudden patter of rain cuts through our silence. The City's drones have fallen, and people turn away from the screened drama, scurrying outside with their mouths open, salt-encrusted faces turned to a new sky as stolen, hoarded water falls in fat drops.

But I stay with the projector. Pause it. Rewind. Back to the falling masonry. Back to one student in particular, whose escape was narrow, almost miraculous.

I see the whites of his eyes underneath dark, curly hair. No bag or other possessions. Only a battered model airplane clutched in one hand.

I watch the brief footage over and over. I study the stoop of his shoulders, the direction of his gaze, the bend of his legs, the quick flex of his arm as he turns to look at his fallen fellow. Will he stay and help, or keep running?

The camera cuts away at the crucial point of Clay's decision.

I rewind, but Big Joan touches my shoulder before I can hit play again.

"Let's travel down to the gates together," she says, "so we can aid whoever makes it out."

Kat Murray is a neurodivergent writer from the San Francisco Bay Area. She spent her early childhood in a counterculture community aboard a boat, and now lives in London with her husband and two children. She has a BA in Journalism from San Francisco State University. When she isn't writing, she's probably gaming, in a forest, or making a cup of tea.

Repurposed Parking Garage

Jacob Coffin

I imagine this building is somewhat well known in this fictional place. I think it was probably converted into living space while the world was busy being a little more post-apoclyptic than solarpunk, with new residents scavenging materials from whatever they could. It's since grown into a sort of community art project, proud of its history, squatters' rights, and the reuse of its materials. The first floor is mixed residential/commercial space (you'd almost have to go out of your way to keep a former parking garage from being handicapped accessible, but I figure some first floor places would make things much easier). The roof is covered in a fruit tree orchard; I used apple, pear, and peach trees, all carefully found and cut out in detail before I completely blasted them to get them to fit the style I was picturing. I figure these are in big planters rather than directly on the surface of the roof. The building can support it, but standing water, especially in places that freeze, can be really bad for buildings, and tree roots can crack concrete just as well as ice.

I thought a lot about the design for the streetcar. I was torn between wanting its purpose to be visually clear at a glance and wanting to show something genuinely strange or futuristic.

I settled on a 1910s-ish streetcar both because it's visually clear and because I think it might be a practical starting point for a society that's trying to rebuild from scratch using entirely local manufacturing. The design is crude, but it's proven—streetcars like this were ubiquitous in the US once upon a time. And they used 1910s-era motors, controls, metallurgy, and manufacturing. It feels like this would be a reasonable starting point, especially with a ready supply of scavenged components and high quality metals laying around above ground in the form of existing vehicles (even wrecks).

I like to imagine that this is a newer phase in this city's public transit infrastructure, that they're starting to standardize their vehicles to simplify things. I like the idea that the first generation of these streetcars would be genuinely a community project, that the city/public transit folks settled on some specifications and devoted their limited budget and manufacturing to producing standardized bases, (the bottom frame, wheels, motors, and pantograph rig) and that people build the carriages out of whatever they have access to. Each streetcar would be a unique, craft-built contraption, sort of 'public transit by way of Weekend Wasteland': all kinds of crazy streetcars made from campers, boats, old school buses, whatever people had access to. City safety inspectors and a committee of local people, with an emphasis on the disabled, would review each one and specify any necessary changes. This gets them a fleet of ready streetcars quickly, allowing them to start providing services while more slowly manufacturing standardized ones to replace the most problematic of the home-built machines.

The slow standardization would be somewhat contentious within a community that took pride in building its own infrastructure, and in the art-like variety. They might chafe at standardization and formalization, like it's a sign that society is stratifying again, though the convenience of a more reliable transit network might help balance it out. As a nod to the artistic spirit and history of the fleet, the new vehicles are painted uniquely by members of the community.

Jacob Coffin is a sci-fi writer with a passion for land conservation, reuse, and the world he lives on not dying. He has previously published with *Metaphorosis Magazine* and *Scrappy Capy Distro*. You can find him at https://jacobcoffinwrites.wordpress.com and on Mastodon at @jacobcoffin@writing.exchange

Icediver

Ruth Joffre

Nothing at the bottom of the ocean bothers her. Nothing natural, that is. On a repair job in the Bering Sea last month, she encountered a lost Japanese spider crab hiking back to the Pacific, following a straight line of radiant heat from the subsea fiber-optic cable she had been dispatched to splice together at a break point. As she stripped the cut cables, the spider crab passed overhead in slow motion, its serene, ponderous movements giving her a chance to study the white ridges of its abdomen and the pinched joints of its legs, which towered over her, much longer than she was tall; harder, too, its reddened carapace reminding her of the skeletons of repair robots designed to scuttle into air ducts and reactor cores to perform dangerous maintenance. Her repair jobs usually mean descending to between 5,000 to 10,000 feet below sea-level—at a depth where the extreme water pressure would collapse a human's lungs. When she dives, her lungs compress, pushing all oxygen into the bloodstream to dissolve. Her gills then open, three delicate slits at the base of her throat opening on each side of her neck to allow seawater to flow over the filaments and oxygenate the blood. Once submerged, her adaptable body temperature and webbed phalanges enable her to live quite comfortably underwater for days or weeks at a time—a capability telecoms were quick to capitalize upon when her species of deep sea dwellers first surfaced about a century ago. Now, Vira jumps at every job opportunity, knowing they will be few and far between.

Her last job was a month ago. Before that, she was living lean off a gig in February.

It's August now, and tourist season in Alaska is less than a month from closing.

Her mother will be out of work again soon.

On the way to pick her mother up from her seasonal job at Kodiak Gulf Floor Tours, Inc., Vira recalculates her September–May budget: $600 per month for her share of the rent for a small two-bedroom apartment she still shares with her mom, $300 per month in student loan payments, $120 per month on average for cell service and the extra data she'll need once she goes over their low limits, another $100 per month to help with gas and car insurance, and about $200 per month for groceries to supplement all the fish she caught, dried, or froze for winter. By her calculations, she has less than $400 left over after bills and necessities to splurge on little gifts for herself, but chances are good her mom will burn right through that with something or other—parking tickets, bail, yet another get-rich-quick scheme that will inevitably blow up in her face.

"Maybe Dave will have something for me," she mutters, pulling into the parking lot.

Once parked, she takes a deep breath, reminding herself, *Be nice. You need the money.*

Dave picks up after barely one ring. "Well, well, well if it isn't my favorite mermaid!"

"I prefer the term sirenx," she reminds him, banging her head inaudibly against the rest.

"Right. Sorry about that." She can hear him wince in discomfort. "So, what's up, Vira?"

She tries not to sound desperate. "I was just calling to see if you have any jobs for me."

He hums, clicking through company portals at his desk to check. "Nothing right now."

His elongated vowels make her think he is hiding something, so she presses. "What about next month? I heard about the plan to build a diverse fiber line on the north side of the Aleutians. Not sure where that is in the process, but I would be happy to install the branching units, like last time." Her head tilts into a joking shrug, even though he can't see her on the phone. "Lord knows they'll need a bunch of branches to hit all the communities on the chain."

"Tell me about it." As a former resident of False Pass, he allows himself a brief moment of bitterness over the delay in extending fiber to his community from the original line festooned on the south side of the Aleutian Chain. "But that project is still in permitting. We're not planning to lay cables until next spring at the earliest. And that's probably aggressive. You know how these things go. It could be five years before anything moves forward. Or six months. Who knows?"

Her forehead rests, dejected, on the steering wheel, but she forces herself to sound casual, like someone who doesn't need this. "I hear ya. Keep me in mind when you do get there, okay?"

"Absolutely. You're at the top of my list, so it's good to know you're interested."

She swallows a lump in her throat. "Definitely. Just tell me when and where."

"Will do. And I'll let you know if anything comes up in the meantime. . . ."

His trailing period makes her think there may be something else, so Vira pauses a second, indulging in the fantasy that he will fill the silence with a job, but she gives up and says goodbye. With a sigh, she hangs up, muttering, "It was a long shot, anyway," into the blank, shining face of the smartphone. Her mother's last tour is scheduled to return in about ten minutes, so Vira leaves her phone in the glove compartment and heads down to the docks in her bathing suit. At this time of year, the water temperatures around Kodiak hover at about 55°F, though they get warmer each passing summer. Most casual swimmers on the shore still wear trunks, but tourists with weighted boots and full-body pressure suits venture farther, with the help of licensed guides, into the frigid depths of the Gulf of Alaska.

Her mother Bárbara is one of the tour guides. Just part sirenx by way of her grandmother on her father's side, Bárbara cannot dive to the same depths as Vira, whose father, a full-blooded sirenx, passed down his gills and compressible lungs before disappearing back under the surface. On the job, Bárbara wears a supplemental oxygen tank, but none of the high-tech gear her clients require. Her uniform consists of a bikini top and a flowing skirt made from seaweed so that when she swims around, her long hair flows behind her in the current, and the tourists think, "Wow, she looks like a mermaid!" A lot of the online reviews for Kodiak Gulf Floor Tours, Inc. read exactly like that. Every once in a while, someone comments, "Would've been better if she wore a tail."

When Vira arrives, her mother hugs her close and whispers, "This is a testy bunch."

With a fake smile for the tourists, Vira asks, "Want me to show off a bit?"

"Could you? I want to end the season on a high note."

Everyone is already looking at Vira by then and pointing their underwater cameras at her. One arm propped on a signpost labeled Gray Whale Watchtower, she asks, "Y'all want a show?" She knows the helmets of their suits have noise-cancelling technology, in order to prevent auditory overstimulation from the engines of cruise ships and recreational boats sailing overhead. Still, the sight of her mouth moving underwater impresses them, and they can tell they are in for a treat. She waves them closer, smiling, then lifts off the gulf floor, twirling and somersaulting like a synchronized swimmer in an Esther Williams movie as their shutters click in unison. Earlier in the season, she might have been joined by gray whales on their migratory path to the Bering Sea. Today, the tourists must settle for some playful sea otters who join her on a lark, their long, sleek bodies corkscrewing through the water.

Sometimes, Vira thinks she has spent her entire life sitting in the audience, waiting, while other people pursue their dreams. As a child, she passed entire summers hanging out on Kodiak's beaches, scanning the horizon for signs of her father, whose human name was Mateo; her mother never did learn his given name or the location of that underwater city she believes he returned to not long after Vira's first birthday. "I got the sense that life down there was rather turbulent," she said once, "and that people back home were expecting him to return and help fix things." Maybe, once the troubles were resolved, he would return, and they could be a family again—at least, that was what Vira hoped. In her fantasies, her father was a tall, well-insulated man, strong enough to carry her around on his shoulders and yet soft enough to hug her and wish her good luck before a swim meet. In ninth grade, she tried out for the high school swim team, thinking that learning the human swim forms would build her endurance for future trips with her father. But almost as soon as the swim coach spotted her webbed fingers and shuttered gills, all hopes were dashed. It would be unfair, the other parents argued, for their children to compete against a merhuman hybrid. She would always have an advantage, they insisted—just look at those toes! Nevermind that Vira had never swum the butterfly in her life. Only after school, when applying for jobs, were her physical adaptations considered a benefit, not a frightening liability.

Employers love cutting costs. One $15,000 repair job for Vira could easily cost a telecom $400,000 once you account for the cost of dispatching the boats, the fuel, the salaries of the crew members—not to mention the collateral damage to businesses reliant on that connectivity and the environment soaking up all that diesel pollution. How much would you pay a merhuman to solve your problems?

"How would you feel if you paid $1,500 and didn't even get a selfie?" Her mother's boss, Benj, flings this question like mud as he follows Bárbara out the front door of the office. All their customers are gone, their tour gear stowed and credit cards charged so they can return to their big cruise ships and luxury hotel rooms, so now Benj and Bárbara are alone but for an administrative assistant blowing bubbles at the desk and Vira, sitting barefoot on the dock, dipping her toes into the gulf. He opens his hand, almost plaintive. "Just think about it from their perspective."

Bárbara stops halfway down the dock and sighs. "I can't control the whales, Benj."

He smiles like someone who has heard this before and had time to fashion a good counter argument for it. "But you do speak their language," he says, "and you can call to them."

"That only works if they're in range." Her arm sweeps out to point northwest. "Most gray whales are all the way on the other side of the Aleutians by now."

"That may be true, but you could at least call to them. Give the tourists a show."

"They won't be able to hear it, anyway." She leans toward him, tapping the wet hair right above her left ear. "Noise-cancelling technology, remember?"

"Careful, Barb. You already have two strikes against you."

"Come on. Be reasonable, Benj. It's the end of the season."

"And I'm trying to make sure we're all still here next season, okay? It's not like we're the only tourist trap in town. These richie rich tourists expect us to pull out all the stops now." Hands on his hips, he shakes his head and turns away from her, scuffing his shoes on the dock. When he spots Vira, he says, "Now here's someone who knows how to put on a real show. Why don't you come work for me, Vira?"

"I don't know, Benj. Will you give me time off for better-paying temp gigs?"

He pushes his lips together and hums disapproval. "Let me think about it."

Once in the car, her mother says, "Sometimes, this job isn't worth it."

Vira waits for a man with sunblock caked on his nose to pass before turning onto the road toward their apartment building. "Pay's decent. And besides, it's only a couple more weeks; then you can hunker down for the winter and catch up on your shows."

"It can't come quickly enough. I'm so tired of people looking at me. Pointing at me." She hangs her head in her hands, then rubs her eyelids with her fingertips. For her, the transition from blinking underwater to walking around in the bright sun often causes bad headaches. Her hybrid eyes must adjust to that light and pressure, the spherical black lenses able to process much more information on the periphery than the flat lenses of humans. In the past, the difficulty of the transition had caused several car accidents after work. Now, Vira picks her mother up and listens to her vent about work five days a week (six during peak season). Bárbara leans back and sighs with closed eyes. "Sometimes, I wish I could disappear. Or that Benj would disappear."

At a stoplight, Vira studies her mother. "I noticed he called you Barb."

"I hate it when he does that. Like we're friends."

Only after they parked did Vira ask, "What did he mean, two strikes?"

"Oh, don't worry, honey. You know how some men love their power trips."

Her mother always says "some men" in order to exclude Mateo from critiques. Even after twenty-four years of complete silence, she still considers him beyond reproach. "Your father was unfailingly kind," she explained once, when Vira asked the fateful question: *Why? Why would he leave us?* "He wouldn't disappear without a good reason. I bet he's out there right now, planning our reunion." This capacity for selective optimism always surprised Vira, who learned at an early age how to interpret her mother's moods. After a long day she liked to be the first one inside their apartment, so she could settle down alone, removing her shoes and socks and massaging that tender spot between the toes where the boots pinched the webbing. On days like this, Vira lingers outside, checking the air pressure in the tires, chatting with the elderly lesbians who live upstairs, considering whether she might hike across the Pacific like that Japanese spider crab and what the consequences would be if she did.

Half an hour later, she decides to head inside, and that's when she finds it: the missed call from Dave, followed by a message saying, *Call me back? I think I've got a job for you....*

Nothing is without risk. Her work is no exception. Once, on a rare multi-week contract to repair fiber-optic spurs off a ring around the North Slope, she dipped under an iceberg floating in the Chukchi Sea and met with the gaping maw of a polar bear hunting in the freezing waters. In a sprint, that sleek white bear was almost as fast, but not nearly as well fed, and she was able to pull away from the mother, whose cub huddled on a nearby iceberg, gnawing at its paws.

From a safe distance, Vira watched the mother surface, sopping wet fur hanging low and thin, like the threadbare strands of seaweed in her mother's work skirt. In emergencies like that, Vira had been instructed to press a gray button in the locator device on her wrist, which served as GPS, beacon, and—if she happened to be in range of a cell tower—a short-range communicator. Some lawyers in tailored suits had devised this precaution to protect her employers from liability, but in reality, such a device was of no use in dangerous situations. A predator could eat, digest, and excrete her before a medevac or rescue crew could reach her. Functionally, the device served one purpose: to alert the company to hire another contractor to complete the job. Thus far, Vira has never pressed that button.

"This job might change that," Dave warns on a call. "It's the riskiest gig I've ever seen."

"That's why you're paying me triple," Vira says. She has already signed the contract; this pre-departure check-in is just a formality, a means of assessing her mental fitness before he signs off on the paperwork, authorizing payment of $50,000 on completion of the assignment.

His breaths whistle slightly, like a deflating balloon. "Are you sure you'll be okay?"

"You know as well as I do I'm the only one who has a hope of surviving at that depth."

"Still. 15,000 feet sounds like a lot. I keep picturing you getting crushed or eaten by some deep-sea leviathan." His voice trembles dramatically, as if narrating the trailer of a black and white B-movie with rudimentary special effects.

"You know my people come from the ocean, right? We've lived there for millennia."

"Technically, we all come from primordial oceans. That's evolution. But this is 2036."

"Yeah, and rent's only getting more expensive. I need this job to pay my internet bill."

He snorts at the astronomical cost of connectivity in rural Alaska. "Good luck with that."

"Does that mean I'm cleared?" She crosses her fingers as she waits for him to say yes.

"Plane'll be there in the morning. 8 AM sharp. It'll take you as far as Chirikof. After that, you'll be on your own." He dwells on this point for longer than she does. "Try to make it back to Kodiak in one piece, okay? I'd hate to have to replace you."

What she promises him and what she promises her mother and herself are entirely different things. Her mother would like her to take this opportunity to seek information about her father and the mysterious city he called home. Bárbara would have her ask each passing mammal if they've seen a merman fitting his description. "About six foot three, brown skin, hair pulled up in a topknot and tied with a ribbon. Once went by the name of Mateo and married a merhuman of mixed Bolivian and white descent—might've talked at length about her legs. Ringing any bells?" Nothing would embarrass Vira more. Beyond fixing the break, her plan for this excursion was simple: explore. Familiarize herself with the terrain. Figure out whether she could survive, not just at this depth, but with the creatures who called it home. Would her lungs implode? Would the bioluminescent squid enchant her into making a home underwater?

A part of her longs for it: the quiet, the freedom from human life.

She barely says a word on the flight to Chirikof. She cannot bear it.

Only after the seaplane drops her off and coasts to shore to refuel does she feel safe. Now the hard work can begin. First, she checks her GPS coordinates, noting her latitude and longitude (55°43'58.7"N 155°31'11.1"W). Her target is approximately thirty-five miles south, near the dark mouth of the Aleutian Trench, where a subsea fiber line connecting Seward, Alaska to Hokkaido, Japan had been placed only nine months prior. *No wonder the company wants to keep this repair quick and quiet*, she thinks, descending into the pitch-black waters of the North Pacific. Here, she wears a full body swimsuit reinforced with Kevlar to protect against shark attacks, a sensor array capable of detecting motion within 150 feet and flashing light at frequencies known to repel apex marine predators, and that all but useless monitor on her wrist, which she continues wearing only because she hates littering and would not leave this trash for her people to clean up.

At no point during the descent does she expect to meet one of her kind.

It comes as a surprise. A flutter of fin on the bottom of her foot. A nibble on her shoulder as she follows the line of broken subsea cable down the jagged slopes of the Aleutian Trench. She flails at the touch and briefly loses her footing. It takes her a moment to calm down.

"Who's there?" She flicks on the floodlight of her headlamp. "Show yourself."

On her second survey of the area, she spots a merperson poking her head out from behind a towering rock spire that may once have been a volcanic vent. With her body hidden by the rock and her hair pulled back into a net adorned with a single seashell, she resembles a dreamy singer-songwriter posing for an album cover in the nineties. "Deep apologies for attempting to eat you," she says. "Your suit makes you look like a seal."

"No worries. Just don't try it again, okay?"

"Okay. My English name is Pod. Do you like the sound? Pod."

"I do," Vira says, dimming the light, "but it's not my place to judge your name."

Pod comes forward to inspect Vira and her lamp. "What name have you chosen?"

"My name was given to me. It's in honor of Viracocha—an ancient Incan deity."

"He who rose from the lake and brought the light," Pod says, as if recalling a textbook.

"How do you know him? I didn't think that the northern and southern merpeople talked."

"We rarely do, but my teacher told us all about him." She circles Vira, studying the straps on her waist, the translucent case of the sensor array that knew before Vira did that Pod was not a predator. She appears to delight in the shortness of Vira's hair and the way it sways in the waters, like stubby strands of brown kelp. Her eyes flash with revelation. "Have you met my teacher? He spent time on land."

"Probably not. Most of the merpeople I've met work for fisheries, reducing bycatch."

Pod sulks a bit and then fixes Vira with wide, iridescent eyes. "Can I trust you?"

This is it, Vira thinks. *I'm finally going to visit an underwater city.* "Yes."

"Good. Now, turn off your lamp," Pod says, offering a hand. In the dark, she guides Vira, warning her about the spines of snailfish, the plumes of hydrothermal vents, the red tentacles of a giant squid passing overhead, its angry black eye fixed on something far off in the distance. First, they walk down the slope, tracing the line of cut fiber. Then, when the rock falls away under them in a sharp cliff, the women begin to swim, following the curve of the cable as it disappears into a recessed cave in the wall of the trench. Someone had to have brought the cable there, Vira thinks. Someone cut it on purpose. All concern as to why dissipates after Pod leads her through a tunnel, into the hollowed mountain she calls home. From a ledge, they look out at a gleaming city full of elaborate spires and shimmery sea glass, illuminated with electricity generated by hydrothermal vents. It expands before them for what seems like miles. "Welcome," Pod says, "to Atxuni."

In one of the few photographs of her father in existence, Vira is still a newborn. A yellow baby blanket swaddles her, so soft and fuzzy that it makes her look like a baby duck with her feet tucked under her feathers for warmth. Her eyes are open, their mottled irises pointed up at Mateo smiling down at her, his face tilted at an angle she cannot remember. Her only memories of her father have been manufactured from photographs like that, with the camera tilted, the light shifted in her mind, so she can believe she was precious to him. *He loved you*, her mother always insisted, but even as a child she picked up on the use of the past tense, as if love was like oxygen: essential on land but quick to dissolve once he slipped under the surface. All her life, even during the summers when she waited for him on the beach, she harbored a bitterness toward him, a hard, unyielding part of herself that accepted none of her mother's high-minded excuses for his sudden departure. *His people needed him. He must have been a great leader, or maybe a doctor.* Early in the tour of Atxuni, Vira asks Pod if she knows anyone by his description, anyone who mentioned becoming a father on the surface, but Pod says no—to her knowledge, no one has left the city for the surface in more than a generation. "Of course, this is not the only city in the trench. There are dozens of others. You should ask there, too."

"Maybe I will," Vira says, knowing this will be a journey for another day.

"Feather might be able to give you a map. Or at least point you in the right direction."

Feather, thinks Vira, imagining a flying fish. "Has everyone here taken English names?"

"Just Feather's students. He came here on an exchange program from one of the Southern Water Cities. He used names to teach us other languages and dialects. In our English unit, no one liked the traditional human names he suggested, so we all decided to invent our own." She rattles off some of the names: *Flame. Rattle. Disco. Optic.*

"I wonder what I would have picked," Vira muses, staring up at a winding spire.

"Ooo, let me guess." Pod considers her for a long moment before saying, "Green tea."

With a laugh, Vira shakes her head. "I was thinking something like Ice. Or—Iceberg."

"Iceberg. Like the lettuce." Vira grimaces, but Pod beams. "Ready to meet Feather?"

Before Vira can respond, Pod parts a curtain of seaweed doubling as a gate and shows her Atxuni's political province, which stretches out before them for the equivalent of several big city blocks before extending up the face of a cliff in five towers carved directly into the rock. Each of the towers rises a hundred or more stories, recalling the skyscrapers Vira has seen only on screen (Kodiak being a relatively short, modest town in comparison to, say, Chicago). At the base of the third tower, Pod says, "We'll have to swim to reach my office." In the water, her body is sinuous and patient, pausing frequently to give Vira time to gaze about in wonder and ask questions, such as: "What are the signs on the sides of the towers?" Pod translates: "These indicate the level and the associated conclave and council. For example, this is the Subduction Refugee and Climate Crisis Conclave. And these next ten levels are the Houses of Grievances and Amends. You might have to visit these to figure out who cut your fiber line and how to fix it."

Treading water, Vira asks, "Should we go now? Make sure this gets on the docket?"

This word, "*docket*", puzzles Pod, and she shakes her head. "No, there is never a line."

"Oh," Vira says, with a self-conscious laugh, then follows Pod up to her office within the Conclave of Edification and Inquiry. Nothing inside the building reminds Vira of an office on the surface—those sad gray boxes people fold themselves into day after day, year after year, as if production was the main goal of their one precious life. Where she expects desks, whiteboards, and rolling chairs, she sees glass bubbles large enough to fit two people, each one outfitted with a screen whose liquid surface ripples like plasma. Most lie dormant, but one displays images on it, which she realizes are projected by a device that resembles the horn of a gramophone. From this, she detects a strange, complex hum, never repeating, impossible to predict. Out of curiosity, Vira calls out to Pod, asking, "What is this?"

Helplessness subsumes Pod's face as she searches for a suitable word. "A . . . telephone?"

"But it sends images," Vira says. She kneels down to better study the mechanics.

"Yes. It . . . encodes and decodes them." Pod points to a resonant tube. "Here."

"Ingenious. It's like our fiber-optic cable, but with directed sound waves."

An unfamiliar male voice behind her says, "An apt observation."

Feather. Pod hugs him and says, "I am glad you are still here. I brought a visitor."

"Hello," Feather says, extending a hand to Vira in a motion that feels novel and practiced, like something he learned in a sociology class about surface-dwellers. "Where are you from?"

"Kodiak." Uncertain if he knows it, she elaborates, "About 200 miles from here."

"You are practically a local, then. Is this your first time to one of our cities?"

Before Vira can nod, Pod interjects, "I found her near the cut fiber line."

No part of this startles him, Vira notes. He says, "I figured they would send someone."

"And here I am." She flaps her arms at her sides, feeling very ordinary, the exact opposite of magnificent in this remarkably shining city. Now that she's here, Vira realizes she would have preferred come to Atxuni in her own time, on her own terms, without the logo of a multi-million-dollar business emblazoned on a device on her wrist; but that isn't the case, and she still has a job to do. She hopes they both understand this. "You wouldn't happen to know who cut the fiber and why, would you? I only ask because they sent me to fix it, and if I do and it gets cut again they're going to get mad, and that could be very bad for me and for the secrecy of this place."

"We are not a secret. We are just too expensive to invade. But your point is taken."

"So . . . do you know who cut the fiber line?" She suspects he never gets his hands dirty.

"I do. Our team worked with engineers from the Conclave of Machinery and Innovation." He explains at a high level the desire to explore methods of transmitting data over long distances, such as the many thousands of miles between Atxuni and the Southern Pacific Water Cities. "We expect this capability will be critical when the climate refugee crisis accelerates."

"And since light travels faster than sound, you want to switch to our fiber technology."

"No." He says this in the firm, decisive tone of one who has already secured consensus in that regard and will not reconsider the matter. "But we were glad of the opportunity to study your technology up close. Until recently, most fiber lines avoided this trench, making a controlled and secure study untenable. This new line allowed us to learn much in a short period of time."

"Does that mean your study is complete? I can repair the line?"

"By all means," he says, with a slight bow of the head.

"No offense, but: do you have the authority to approve that?"

Feather and Pod exchange quizzical looks. "I am the Primary of the Conclave," he begins by way of explaining his position. "To you, that would be akin to the head of a major department in your nation's government."

"Like the Secretary of Education."

"Precisely."

"But you said another conclave was involved?"

"In cases of collaboration and partnership, the one speaks for the whole."

What she says is, "Okay," but what she thinks to herself is, *That sounds like a really good way to silence dissent and create a false sense of unity.* That does not seem to be Feather's intent, but she is wary of believing Atxuni to be perfect, idealizing a place she has never lived because it appears to have solved problems no one can even be bothered to acknowledge in her society. She sighs at the thought of going back, but it must be done. She has a job to do, but she doesn't know how to say goodbye. "Well, that solves that. No need to go to the House of Grievances, after all."

"Oh no." Pod's voice deflates with disappointment. "You're not leaving already?"

"It's a long swim back. I should probably just fix the line and get going."

"No, no," Feather and Pod say in unison. He assures Vira, "We can speak to the Conclave of Transportation about chartering a submarine. It will cut your journey down considerably."

"Are you sure? That sounds expensive. And it's really not necessary. I can manage."

"We insist," Pod says. "You are our cousin from the surface. You should see the city."

"And I know a team of engineers who would love to talk to a technician of your caliber."

"I'm basically a mechanic with strong lungs," she says, knowing they will protest, feeling perhaps for the first time in her life that she might be more than just a telecom tech, a gig worker, perpetually at the mercy of the economy and the vicissitudes of executive decision making. Here in Atxuni, her unique talents matter more than they ever have before and perhaps ever will again. She agrees to speak with the civic engineers about their plans for longitudinal transmission tubes. Over dinner, they discuss fault lines, hydrothermal capture, the manner in which kelp or seaweed can be processed and extruded into delicate beds of noodles for the raw fish slices served to them on plates of smoothed sea glass. Floating down an alley, marveling at the intricate tile mosaics of squid and spiny dogfish, she finds herself thinking, *I could live here*, then stopping herself with a familiar question: *What about Bárbara?*

On the submarine ride to Kodiak, she studies the holographic map Feather gave her of the Northern Pacific Water Cities, which stretch across the vast expanse of the ocean from Tokyo in the west to Panama City in the east, from the Aleutian Trench in the north to the equator dividing north and south. It would take years—decades, even—to search these Water Cities for her father Mateo, and there would be no guarantee of finding him. She could be in the same city as him, rest on a bench as he swims overhead mere feet away, and still miss him. He could be in Atxuni right now, going on with his life without her. Her father, the abandoner. Only after Feather handed her the map Pod promised did Vira realize part of her was invested in the fantasy that Pod was going to accidentally reintroduce her to Mateo; that theirs was to be a narrative of coincidence, reunion, maybe even forgiveness—but that is not this story, she admits. That is just her seeking an answer to a question asked long ago: *Why did he leave me?*

Her submarine pilot asks a better question: "Are you planning to return to Atxuni?"

"I think so. I'm not sure when, though. I have a lot of things to take care of."

He hums his understanding. "Is life on the surface very complicated?"

"Very." Not wanting to think about it, she turns to watch the submarine's mechanical fins gliding effortlessly though the cold water. Forward and back, forward, back. Unlike human-made submarines, with their tin-can aesthetic, mersubmarines were shaped like humpback whales, with extended pectoral fins and a soft, slumped belly, allowing the sub to curve and to circulate water. Like most mertech, the sub was powered by a combination of trapped hydrothermal energy and a perpetual circulation machine activated by ocean currents. Out of the water, the sub, like the holo map Feather provided, would cease to function. She zooms in again on the Aleutian Trench cities and asks the pilot, "Are all water cities as beautiful as Atxuni?"

"All the ones I've been to. Some even more so."

"Which one would you recommend visiting?"

"For you? Qirz. It's a domed city with waterfalls and beautiful gardens; their Conclave of Hybridity has done wondrous things marrying mertech and human mechanical engineering."

"It sounds like they should be overseeing the longitudinal transmission project."

"Oh, all the trench cities work together. But Atxuni was closest to the fiber."

"Makes sense," she says, though she has more questions than time to ask them.

The pilot pulls up in front of Gray Whale Watchtower, and Vira has to say goodbye.

Almost as soon as she sets foot on Kodiak, dread seeps into her heart, heavy and familiar. How will she explain her experience in Atxuni to Bárbara? And should she even try? Her mother cannot survive at such depths. She cannot swim that trench or embark on an endless quest to find Mateo—that gilded, glorious image she manufactured of him so that he could never possibly live up to her expectations. Still, if there was any possibility of reuniting with her long lost lover, Bárbara would have taken it without question. On bad nights when Vira was just a kid and had to peel her mother out of a depression in the couch, Bárbara would sneer, "I shoulda sent you to live at your cousin's in the Lower 48; then I wouldn't be in this mess." This mess meaning the trappings of paying for an apartment and a mouth to feed, plus whatever trouble she had gotten herself into drinking or gambling. If Bárbara knew Vira had a connection to Atxuni, she would try her best to capitalize on it. Arrange submarine tours. Bring back mertech.

No, decides Vira. She will not tell Bárbara what happened.

Before heading home, she stops at Dave's office to return her locator device and check on throughput post-repair. "Another excellent job, Vira—we're back up to a total of five terabits per second," he boasts, pointing to real-time data visualizations on his screen. Hair still dripping over her right shoulder, she watches Dave perform the final tests to confirm satisfactory completion of the job. While he completes the requisite forms, he asks a question for which she has prepared an answer: "So, what do you think did it?"

"Earthquake debris. You know how volatile the Aleutians are. Surprised you built there."

"Yeah, well." He shrugged, filing the paperwork away. "That's above my paygrade."

With a laugh, she says goodbye with a wave. "Call me next time it breaks."

He nods and salutes her with two fingers. "You got it."

Outside, Vira pauses to enjoy the warm sun on her dry clothes and the $50,000 super rush job rate soon to hit her bank account. With that kind of money, she could take the rest of the year off and explore the other trench cities on Feather's holo map. As she walks home in the perpetual August light she thinks, *I just might.* Why not? She's young—just twenty-three going on twenty-four—and she's grown tired of Kodiak, the high cost of milk, the looks white people in particular give her when they notice her gills. For the first time, she thinks she knows what made her father abandon his new family.

He wasn't a hero, she realizes. He just wanted to feel like he belonged.

Ruth Joffre is the author of the story collection *Night Beast*. Her work has appeared or is forthcoming in *Lightspeed*, *Nightmare*, *Pleiades*, *khōréō*, *The Florida Review Online*, *Wigleaf*, *Baffling Magazine*, and the anthologies *Best Microfiction 2021 & 2022*, *Unfettered Hexes: Queer Tales of Insatiable Darkness*, and *Evergreen: Grim Tales & Verses from the Gloomy Northwest*.

SQUAWKER AND DOLPHIN SWIMMING TOGETHER

T.K. Rex

The Submersible aQuatic Cetacean Communication Robot—professionally known as SQCCR, affectionately known as "Squawker"—splashes into the harbor from the starboard side of the Charlotte's Web at dawn. A few brilliant, cool drops hit Julia's skin.

The heat index is already 96 and aiming for the red by ten. What must the dolphins think of the extra three degrees the world's gained since the oldest members of their pods were born?

Maybe this is the upgrade that will finally help her find out.

"Everything's looking good," Parviz says through the radio, from his station by the monitors back at the lab. "Hey I'm hearing some signature whistles—it's the ladies. They're not too far from you."

Julia scans the gentle blue-green waves for them, from the causeway in the distance to the houseboats down in Punta Gorda, where there were houses just ten years ago.

"There they are!" Tumelo says, pointing west with their chin. Julia's grad student from Botswana is taller than her, even more than most people are, with a frohawk, a kind heart, and a gift for training AI on real-world data.

Julia can see the pod, dorsal fins cutting through the shining surface of the bay, spouts and splashes getting closer. Parviz comes in on radio, "Whoa, they're already approaching. That was fast."

Time to get back to the lab. She misses the days of working directly with the dolphins, but it's better for them this way.

As the *Charlotte's Web* turns around and picks up speed, she catches a glimpse of them below the surface. Ten female Atlantic bottlenose dolphins, gray and sleek and strong, with their three calves. The mammals swim against and around each other, close and then apart and close again, one leaps, another leaps, three more surface to exhale.

Tumelo grins wide at Julia, then looks back out at the water, where just below the surface a dolphin is already swimming right up to the drone. "That must be Summer," Tumelo says.

Julia nods. Summer's the only one who hasn't lost interest in Squawker.

Parviz confirms. “She’s definitely saying something—” A few clicks and whistles filter through his pause. “It’s processing....” It’s not physically possible to be any sweatier, but Julia’s palms somehow feel even slicker than they did a minute ago. Is this it? “Oh shit,” Parviz says. “The new visuals are way better.”

Julia’s heart pounds in her chest like a storm. Tumelo grabs her arm, grip strong and smile wide.

“What are you seeing?!” Julia asks Parviz.

“Uhh...It’s kind of football shaped...with...wings? It looks like Squawker! Those are its solar panels, holy shit! It looks a *lot* like Squawker. She’s literally sending us a portrait. It’s crystal clear, Jules. Damn. We nailed it this time.” There’s victory and wonder in his voice.

Tumelo jumps up and down with excitement. “Yes! We finally did it! Oh, I would hug you if it wasn’t so hot!”

Julia laughs and cheers with her team. Two decades of work have led to this. The hardware, the algorithms, the past three years of fine-tuning...all so she could see the dolphins’ sounds the way the dolphins do, in three dimensions. She can’t wait to get back to the lab and look at the results herself.

After a lifetime of wondering, she’s finally going to know exactly what they’re saying.

What will she say back?

That night, instead of going home, they look at all the footage and the readouts from the afternoon another dozen times. Tumelo picks up samosas and biryani from the place across the street and Anusha brings Prosecco. Parviz runs ’30s hip hop through the visualizer until Anusha drives him home. By 2am Tumelo and Julia are still there, looking over everything, just one more time.

“Right here,” Tumelo says, pointing at a monitor. “That’s the drone.”

“I wonder,” Julia says, leaning on the back of Tumelo’s chair, “if we have enough data with this yet to compose an original message. Not just mimicry.”

“Oh.” They nod enthusiastically. “I think we do. We’ve got the drone, and the dolphin, and the boat, and I still think those things are fish.... And then there’s all this stuff that we just have no idea what it is." They grin, gesturing to the incomprehensible forms swirling on the third monitor.

"What do you think of it?" Julia asks. "Honestly."

"I think . . . it's beautiful. It could be pure expression, play, something we're not calibrated for . . . ."

"Abstraction?"

Tumelo laughs. "Anusha definitely thinks so."

"But do *you* think so? *Tursiops* has been around at least five million years, and the dolphin braincase has barely changed in twelve million. They've had the biology to communicate with this level of complexity six times longer than we've been capable of spoken language. We *know* they have the mental capacity. We *know* they're capable of abstract thought. And now we finally have a way of teasing out which words are literal representations of our world, and which aren't. *Those* are the ones I want to understand next, Tumelo."

"I'm with you, Dr. Redhearth. It's all very exciting."

Julia swallows the last of her warm prosecco. "You're bilingual."

"Trilingual, actually," Tumelo grins. "Why?"

"Nice. So you know how learning a new language expands the way you see the world, the concepts you have access to."

"Oh, definitely."

"Imagine what new concepts they could bring into our world, Tumelo."

"Or us to theirs, Dr. Redhearth."

True. Julia nods and thinks of all the trash in Charlotte Harbor. All the violence in the news. The extremists and the propaganda, the dead zones in the Gulf. . . . But maybe . . . maybe an outside perspective is just the thing the human world needs.

Or another glass of Prosecco. She pours the last splash of the last bottle out into each of their mugs. "To Summer."

"To Summer," Tumelo smiles warmly.

It's room temperature and flat. What had they been talking about before the dread seeped in? Something about how long dolphins have been capable of language. "You know," Julia says, swirling her mug, "they've had time to evolve their languages into things we might not even understand. Nam-shubs, obscure allegories, ways of communicating we've only imagined in science fiction."

"Look at you, Dr. Redhearth, getting into the telepathic dolphin comment thread! If the Redditors could see you now!"

Julia laughs heartily. "I am *not* saying they're telepathic! But since you went there, we know they can target sound like a laser beam, right? So what's stopping them from triggering the speech centers of the brain directly and making us hear English words, with enough practice? I'm just saying!"

"You're just tipsy, is what you are!"

"That. Is true."

"Listen, Julia. Tomorrow, I'm going to start composing our first original animation. And we're going to finally prove to Summer that our little Squawker isn't just a novelty. And then, one piece at a time, we'll figure out what all that other . . . *stuff* . . . is. Tonight, you better call a car, OK?"

"Tomorrow's Saturday."

"And?"

The whole team is at the research center, glued to the monitors streaming Squawker's feed. Summer's smooth, gray form fills the video, and her usual chatter streams in through the speakers. It'll take time to process that part of the conversation, but right now, Julia is trying to remember to breathe, palms sweating, waiting for a momentary lull in Summer's monologue to press the button. To share, for the first time, something in Summer's language that isn't merely mimicry.

And then it's there, the break, and Summer waits. Usually this is when they play what she just said back to her, and they go back and forth until she gets bored or the other dolphins call her away. But this time, Julia hits the key that plays the statement they spent a solid week composing out of scraps of sound, testing and retesting to make sure it reproduced in three dimensions as intended.

On the screen, it looks like what she hopes Summer sees: a 3D rendering of Squawker and a dolphin in motion, swimming together. The computer generates the caption: SQUAWKER AND DOLPHIN SWIMMING TOGETHER. The sound is only squeaks, indistinguishable to Julia's ears from thousands she's heard before, most of it outside her hearing range entirely.

What follows is a moment of curious silence, Summer turning her head to look at Squawker closely with one eye, then swimming around it, examining it the way she did the first time she met the drone two years ago. The gathered scientists all hold their breath.

Then a barrage of squeaks and whistles, and Julia thinks she recognizes the same squeak they just sent, repeated several times, but she can't be sure.

The translation comes in. A perfect 3D rendering of Squawker and a dolphin swimming side by side. The machine translation captions: SQUAWKER AND DOLPHIN SWIMMING TOGETHER.

There's so much to analyze here, Julia's thinking, as a murmur rises, and becomes a cheer, and Parviz high-fives everybody. Tumelo, grinning wide, asks Julia if they should draft a press release.

Before Julia can even wrap her head around that, Summer swims away abruptly.

"Oh shit, we didn't scare her off, did we?" Parviz asks.

"Not this dolphin—she's fearless," says Tumelo.

"She's telling the pod. Look," Anusha says, and points to the Camera 5 monitor with a slender hand and an eager sparkle in her black-lined eyes. In the distance, Summer joins the pod, and the speakers around the room play their faint, far away chatter.

Julia is certain she hears sounds that make up SQUAWKER AND DOLPHIN SWIMMING TOGETHER repeated among the pod. Summer's telling them what the drone said, she has to be.

It's working. Real communication is finally possible. The weight of so many years of doubt starts lifting.

But what happens now? For a moment she feels almost dizzy.

The pod follows Summer back to Squawker. Summer whistles at the drone, and Julia would give anything to know what she's saying right now, but there's a short delay in processing. For now, there's only one response. Julia hits send.

SQUAWKER AND DOLPHIN SWIMMING TOGETHER.

The pod erupts in chatter. So many speaking so fast simultaneously they'll never pick it all apart.

Later, analyzing everything, Summer's parting phrase that day stands out. It's a vivid image of herself and Squawker swimming side by side, just like in the message they sent, but now surrounded by the pod. In the recording, Squawker has no reply. But Summer waits. She waits until the pod begins to leave, and call for her, and then she finally, slowly, turns and swims away.

POD SWIMMING. FISH. POD CHASING FISH. CATCHING FISH. EATING FISH. SQUAWKER EATING FISH.

Julia only has so many phrases to respond with. She pulls up the new VR interface Parviz designed and adds a file from the weather category they explored last week.

SQUAWKER EATING SUN. She makes up for the drone's lack of a mouth by simply having it absorb the sun, swallowing it whole through its solar panel fins.

Summer gives the drone a sort of side-eye. SUN, she repeats. Incredulous, maybe? Then a string the computer isn't confident about but might be a dolphin jumping so high it gets lost in the clouds. Julia laughs. That can't be it, but wow. It's almost a joke, almost a fable. Could they really have those? Anything is starting to seem possible.

In a stroke of insight, she commands the drone to surface and start charging up its solar fins. Through its cameras, Julia floats virtually upward through the green, wet world that surrounds her in VR. Summer follows, chattering so many things so fast the computer can't keep up. When the fins unfurl, Summer squeaks, and the computer catches: SQUAWKER EATING SUN. SQUAWKER EATING SUN. SQUAWKER EATING SUN.

Julia wants to try something else, just to see Summer's reaction. The human form she picks is a bit of public domain 3D clip art, a blonde woman in a bikini, frozen in a front crawl stroke.

Summer responds with an image of the woman falling into Squawker's solar panels, like the sun did earlier. The machine translation makes her laugh out loud: SQUAWKER EATING HUMAN.

Julia tries to think of a response, but Summer has more to say first: HUMAN, BOAT, [UNINTELLIGIBLE]. NETS. FISH GOING UP. [UNINTELLIGIBLE] DOLPHINS AND HUMANS SWIMMING TOGETHER. [UNINTELLIGIBLE] HUMAN SHOOTING AT DOLPHINS FROM BOAT.

The last image isn't one she's seen before from Summer, but it's clear as day, the gun is there in the man's hands and the shockwave of the gunshots distorts the whole thing in a sudden burst. The machine translation is dead on.

A few years ago some drunk asshole took his motorboat out into the harbor and started shooting at the dolphins playing in his wake. Two females were injured, and a calf was killed. Julia was livid. The whole mess sped up the team's decision to use drones exclusively, to keep the dolphins from expecting anything but wakes from boats.

Summer's expression of the event chills Julia. Not just because they both remember the same painful incident, and not just because it's finally proof dolphins can translate what they see above the water into 3D burst-pulse language. The thing that feels like a storm surge on a doorstep is the fact it wasn't even Summer's pod.

And Summer isn't done. DOLPHINS SINKING. [UNINTELLIGIBLE]. She claps her jaw, flashing pointed teeth.

That's a threat behavior. Julia replies with: DOLPHIN SWIMMING. SQUAWKER SWIMMING. How to convey an absence? A big 3D "X" over the human? Ha.

Summer replies before she can come up with anything, adding her own signature whistle to the established dolphin form: SUMMER-DOLPHIN AND SQUAWKER SWIMMING TOGETHER. She doesn't mention humans.

"Some of us have been real dicks, haven't we?" she mutters to the monitors. The shooter in the motorboat didn't go to jail. He didn't lose his boat. He didn't even lose his gun. She wants to believe that would have gone differently if it had been a human child killed, but this is Florida, after all.

She tries to keep the abstract as downplayed as possible, but everyone sees through it. The moment it's up on the conference website, Julia starts getting messages from colleagues.

"You did it, didn't you?"

"Is this what I think it is?"

"Holy shit, I can't wait to see this talk."

"I'm literally imagining you showing up on that stage with a dolphin in some kind of land suit, please tell me that's your plan, Julia!"

Even the most well-meaning responses from people she's known for years make her palms sweat when she sees them.

She's jet lagged from the flight to Vancouver, and nervous on the stage the way she always is, but when Summer's picture comes up on the screen she can't help but smile.

"And that's Summer, interacting with our drone this past July, a few weeks after the upgrades. And now I'll play some clips from our conversation that day."

She goes to the next slide, and the squeaks and buzzes of burst-pulses fill the hall from every speaker, while the 3D animation of their meaning plays, overlaid on the video of Summer holding a fish between her teeth. FISH, the caption says, with Summer's perfect 3D render of the creature she just caught. FISH, the drone repeats. They do the same with SNAIL, BEER CAN, and SCALLOP.

After apparently finishing the lesson to Summer's satisfaction, Squawker says, CHRYSANTHEMUM. Tumelo made the 3D render from a scan they'd taken at a diner table when the team was out lunch.

"We wanted to see what she would do with something she's never observed before."

Summer swims away.

"Wait for it...."

She comes back a moment later with a sea urchin clinging to a frayed yard of orange rope. It does resemble the chrysanthemum, as much as anything in Charlotte Harbor. The crowd laughs, then starts applauding.

By the time her talk is over and the line for questions stretches to the door, she feels the first sprinkle of accomplishment set in like cooling rain. Her cheeks begin to ache from smiling.

She calls on the first person in line, one of the young cynics who gave a talk last year on how it's probably all pretty nonsense, just like birdsong.

"All the so-called 'words' you've shown us today are still basically mimicry," he says. "No different from a lyre bird replicating the sound of a chainsaw. So, I applaud you for finally getting these images into focus, but is there any indication in any of this that the dolphins are doing anything but playing?"

And what's so wrong with that? Deep breath, Julia. Be nice.

"There is," she answers calmly. "Most of what we're picking up from the rest of the pod is still unintelligible. Can we definitively say everything we don't understand is something profound? Of course not. A lot of it is probably gossip, which we know humans use for social bonding. Some of it is probably fun nonsense, the way we make up words when we sing. The big breakthrough here is that now, with a few words we do understand, we can start to learn the rest. Next question."

An older academic she's met a couple times at other conferences is next. “Well, this is more of a comment than a question.” A few groans come from the audience. “This research is very interesting, and if it can be successfully replicated with more than one dolphin, I have to say it seems like it might be enough to start seeking legal personhood again.” A few people clap, most nod.

“You might be right. I hope you’re right.” Julia shrugs and smiles. “Who knows, maybe this time next year it’ll be Summer up here doing the presenting.”

Polite laughter. Everyone here knows it’ll be years before they understand the language enough for Summer or some other dolphin to declare their personhood, without ambiguity, in any court of law with heft. And even then, laws can be fickle.

The whole team gathers after, greeting her with high fives and hugs outside the conference center. “Drinks on me!” Parviz declares, and belts out a sea shanty as they walk along Vancouver Harbor to the hotel bar.

Oh what do you do with a talking dolphin?
What do you do with a talking dolphin?
What do you do with a talking dolphin?
Register her to voooote

Anusha, still laughing at Parviz’s antics, stops and leans over the rail, pointing out at the water. “Look, orcas!”

They stop and look. Julia sees a spout, then three tall black dorsal fins, out near the bare wood spires of a sunken forest. It was still an island last time she was here.

Tumelo declares heartily, “They send their congratulations, Dr. Redhearth!”

“I wonder if we could explain all this somehow to Summer when we get back?” Anusha muses, tracing a slow line across the condensation of her beer glass. The water drips onto the reclaimed wood of their corner table.

Behind Anusha at the bar are two young men loudly exalting some new product called a “dronephone,” and an enormous television playing local news, both of which Julia has more or less successfully ignored all night.

"Yes! I could throw together a whole sequence for her," Tumelo says. "I wonder how much of it would make sense to her though?"

"I bet she thinks airplanes are some kind of bird," Parviz says.

Anusha laughs a little. "I think she knows they're machines. When they fly low? All that noise? Come on."

"But does she know what a machine is? Does she know Squawker is a machine?" Parviz counters, and finishes his third glass.

The television centers in on Florida. Julia remembers it's world news, and grits her teeth, expecting what comes next. A red trajectory cone that was pointed at the panhandle yesterday has shifted south. Way south.

"Shit."

The team follows her gaze, past the young men, one of whom loudly explains to the other, "Remember the little guys that followed you around in those old MMOs? It's like that, but, like, with tentacles. We're gonna make so much fuckin' money."

"Hey!" Anusha yells. "Shut up for a second!"

There's a brief lull, where both men visibly consider hitting on Anusha, then decide better of it when they see Julia's glare.

The meteorologist's voice finally finds its way across the bar to them. "This might remind some of our older viewers of what happened with Ian in '22, and Charley way back in '04. Those were smaller hurricanes by today's standards, but—"

"Checking our flight," Parviz already has his phone out. A moment later they get the notification: canceled.

"What do we do?" Tumelo asks. "I'm from a landlocked country."

"Do we have someone who can go to the lab and get the hurricane shutters down?" Anusha asks.

Julia nods, already swiping through her contacts.

The room she's splitting with Anusha has two oversized blue beds, stylized wall art of orcas and salmon by a local Squamish printmaker, and an inset television that takes up most of the widest wall.

All they can do is watch.

Watch as the too-warm water of the Gulf of Mexico feeds the

hurricane enough to grow from category four to category five.

And in the morning, after barely sleeping, they watch, still in their pajamas, Anusha's hand over her mouth in shock, Julia too frozen with her arm around Anusha to answer Tumelo's knock on their door, as a category six makes landfall.

Julia's mom has a hundred million mugs. There's one from their Grand Canyon trip when she was nine, one each from all five tech companies Mom built apps for in the '20s, and of course the one from Bermuda that Julia gave her when she went for research as a grad student. There's a dolphin on it. Like her favorite Florida mug back at the lab. The one that's probably at the bottom of Charlotte Harbor now with everything else.

Julia pushes the dolphin mug back into the crowded cupboard and grabs the two handmade ones they found at a garage sale once when she was seventeen. She fills them up with coffee and meets Mom on the side deck, where the late-spring sun has warmed the air enough that she can barely see the steam rise off their drinks.

"Ooh, you brought coffee! See, this is why you're my favorite."

"Ha. I'm your only." She can't quite bring herself to smile back, but she tries.

"You know, I think I saw a fluke out there," Mom says, pointing with her chin while she cups the hot mug with both hands. "Couple spouts."

To the west, past a swathe of blooming coastal prairie and a grove of twisty windblown pines, the cold Pacific Ocean crashes into the state of Oregon, gnawing off a chunk with every wave.

Julia grunts, and sips her coffee, leaning back into the wooden deck chair.

"You know," Mom says, "they still do those whale watching trips I used to take you on in town. Different folks running it, nice couple though. I could book us—"

"Mom, stop. I don't want to go whale watching."

"I know." Mom sighs. "You're depressed. I get it." She sets her mug down on the little rusting table that she's kept out here for twenty years. "But honey, this is your life's work. You've got to get back up on your feet. It's been six months."

"Are you sick of me already?"

"Never! But Julia, seriously. There has to be something you can do instead of sitting around here playing video games all day."

"I'm not. . . ." Who is she kidding? Every few days she brings out a VR headset with the intention of re-watching Squawker's old recordings, the ones saved to the cloud, taking notes or something, maybe getting a new insight. But every time she puts it on, she stares at the folder for a few minutes, and inevitably opens *Elder Scrolls VII* instead, where she can be a hot elf mage with easily definable and imminently achievable problems to solve for the rest of the day.

"Yeah, I thought so," Mom replies to Julia's trailed-off thought.

DOLPHIN SINKING.

"What's the point, Mom? What's the fucking point of trying to talk to dolphins when people are killed and displaced by the millions in these floods, and storms, and fires, and plagues? Every fucking year. I should be helping with the rewilding efforts out here, or doing climate science, or joining the protests or doing eco-terrorism, anything, anything that actually might help slow this planet's fucking freefall."

"Honey," Mom says, "leave the 'eco-terrorism' to the pros." She winks. Julia suddenly wonders where she really was last week, but before she can finish that thought, Mom continues. "I can't believe I'm the one who has to tell you this, but dolphins are people too. And we share the same fucked up world. And *they still need you.*"

How can I help anybody when I'm the one drowning?

Julia's phone vibrates in the pocket of her sweatpants. She sighs and takes a peek. Parviz. He's been volunteering with the recovery effort since it started, texting her photos every few days that she can't bear to look at. But this time it's a phone call.

"Answer it!" Mom says.

She rolls her eyes, and does.

"Jules!" Parviz sounds different. Brighter. Sober. "You're not gonna believe it. We found Squawker!"

The *Charlotte's Web*, patched up from its encounter with a downtown Punta Gorda sports bar, sputters to a slow drift near the debris-strewn strip of sand that was Boca Grande a year ago.

Parviz leans on the rail by Julia, joining her in awe of the destruction. There are no words for it.

But it's not why they're here.

"Wish Tumelo was with us for this," he says.

"I'm working on their visa," Julia replies, brushing a windblown curl out of her eyes.

"You know if we can't get them back soon, one of the elephant teams will snatch them up. Or those weird tree people. Or—"

"I know. If this is our pod, maybe we can get some funding, speed it up a little."

Assuming the pod made it through the storm. Assuming Summer, or any of them, still remembers Squawker. Assuming any dolphin gives a shit and has the patience to start teaching them again.

"Hey!" Anusha yells from the cabin, pulling her headphones to the side. "I got the signature whistles! Three matches so far!"

If one of them was Summer, Anusha would have said so. Julia's heart starts pounding anyway. Any familiar dolphin is better than none, and they were all interested in Squawker at first. Maybe's it's been long enough that the novelty effect will work again.

But Summer. . . . She might still turn up. No reason to assume the worst.

"There they are!" Parviz points and grins wide.

Julia sees them. Three dorsal fins slip through the water, then another two, one so small it's barely visible. A new calf.

She wonders what the little one's signature whistle sounds like.

"They're gonna be so stoked to see Squawker again," Parviz says.

Where's Summer?

When the drone is in the water, Julia heads to the cabin, where Anusha hands her the headset and makes room on the small bench. Their new onboard equipment is a joke compared to what they lost, but it's all they can afford for now, and the *Charlotte's Web* is the closest thing they have left to a lab.

Through Squawker's cameras, she sees the dolphins in the distance. And the rubble on the sea floor, stretching as far as the blue-gray visibility allows today. Mailboxes, planks of wood, entire cars, palm trees with dead algae-laden fronds still on them, swaying in the current where they stick out from the sand.

And a few fish. Maybe, if the Gulf wasn't too warm and too acidic, a coral reef would grow out of the ruins, over time.

She sends out a call to the pod, an image of Squawker. Maybe someone will recognize it.

A couple of dolphins turn to look, and she's hit with a barrage of echolocation clicks. One swims toward her, fast.

The rendered visuals are low poly and the translation lags, but the message is unmistakable.

SUMMER-DOLPHIN AND SQUAWKER SWIMMING TOGETHER.

It's her. Julia catches her relief in her throat. "It's Summer!" she says out loud, and sends Summer's message back as quickly as she can. Parviz and Anusha cheer.

"I'm texting Tumelo!" Anusha says.

Summer slides against the drone excitedly, knocking it off-kilter for a moment in a dolphin version of a bear hug. Then she hovers in the water, in front of Squawker's front cameras, and unloads.

SUMMER-DOLPHIN SWIMMING [UNINTELLIGIBLE]. SHARKS EATING SQUAWKER. SQUAWKER CAUGHT IN NET. BOAT EATING SQUAWKER. HUMAN SHOOTING SQUAWKER.

Was she . . . worried about the drone? She goes on.

SUMMER-DOLPHIN ALONE, SWIMMING IN EVERY DIRECTION [LOW CONFIDENCE]. [UNINTELLIGIBLE]. BOATS SINKING. [UNINTELLIGIBLE]. HUMANS SINKING. DEBRIS [LOW CONFIDENCE] SINKING. TREES SINKING.

There's a layer to the visuals that looks like something from the weather category. This is what the hurricane was like for her, it has to be.

Summer still isn't done. SUMMER-DOLPHIN [UNINTELLIGIBLE] SQUAWKER. SUMMER-DOLPHIN LIFTING SQUAWKER TO THE SURFACE. [UNINTELLIGIBLE]. SQUAWKER [UNINTELLIGIBLE]. SQUAWKER SINKING. SUMMER-DOLPHIN [UNINTELLIGIBLE]. SUMMER-DOLPHIN PUSHING SQUAWKER TO LAND. SUMMER-DOLPHIN SWIMMING ALONE. [UNINTELLIGIBLE]. SUMMER-DOLPHIN WITH POD [UNINTELLIGIBLE].

"Damn, Summer." Parviz says. He must be watching the cabin monitor. "Am I seeing this right? Did she go looking for Squawker after the storm and . . . ."

"She tried to help it by lifting it up to the surface," Anusha says, in awe. "It's what she would do with a sick calf, but . . . she also knows Squawker eats sunlight."

"And then when Squawker still wouldn't talk to her, she brought it to shore," Julia says.

"Maybe thinking humans could help it?" Anusha wonders. "Maybe she knows we made it after all."

"We found Squawker on the beach near the lab," Parviz says. "Fuck. This explains why no one noticed it on the first pass. She hadn't rescued it yet."

It takes a moment to sink in.

"How do dolphins thank each other?" Julia breathes.

No one has an answer. Not yet. Not for years, if years are something they still have.

She has far more to thank Summer for than just saving Squawker.

Getting back out here, facing their ruined equipment, the ruined lives and homes. Joining Parviz and Anusha in the volunteer efforts while they were waiting for the boat's repairs. Seeing the restaurant owners and fishermen and the people from the laundromat, the neighbors of the lab who she never gave a second thought to before, all working together to rebuild, stopping in the rubble to contain their sudden tears. She only came back to be a part of that because Summer saved her drone.

Summer's endless patience, curiosity, collaboration . . . they've kept Julia afloat so many times.

And the simple fact that Summer's always seemed to want to learn, to bridge the gap between them, just as much Julia . . . .

She leans against the hard wall of the cabin and bites her lower lip to hold back the tide of feelings.

Summer waits for her response, head cocked, eyes searching the cameras.

T. K. Rex is a science fiction and fantasy author from the western states, whose stories can be read in more than forty publications, including *The Sunday Morning Transport*, *Apex*, *Asimov's*, and their debut collection, *The Wildcraft Drones*, coming 2026. They're an alumni of the Clarion, Taos Toolbox and Futurescapes workshops; a member of the Science Fiction & Fantasy Writers Association, the Authors Guild, and the Writers Grotto; the co-host of Stir, a reading series in San Francisco; and ADHD as hell. T. K.'s stories, socials, and newsletter can be found at tkrex.wtf.

Swimming Whole

E. C. Barrett

First Jeff Martin bought the narrow strip of land between the river and Banks Road from the town, then he spider-webbed caution tape between the trees and nailed posted signs to their bark. The swimming hole where so many of us had spent our childhood summers was no longer ours. And this with each year hotter than the last.

Martin, who also owned *The Weekly Gazette*, the Dollar Store on the edge of town, and a quarter of the rental properties, bought and moved into the Carter Mansion across the street from our swimming hole after the last owner died. As big as it was, it wouldn't pass as a mansion nowadays, but the historical plaque in front of it named it the original home of the town founder. A draw, no doubt, for Martin, who fancied himself a self-made man in the way the wealthy who grew up just shy of wealthy tend to do. He didn't live there one full summer before he convinced the town council that the strip of land—the only spot with passable access down the river-cut gorge—was nothing more than a waste of taxpayer money.

Why pay to have it mown, when he could send his landscape crew over? (And seeing as he was doing the town this favor, really, the property ought to be tax-exempt, didn't they agree?) Like most things Jeff Martin said and did, it had the sound of a gift bestowed. Like everything he said and did, the beneficiary was definitively him.

How many generations had we kept that spot a secret from the June-to-August tourists who crowded the lake beach and left their soda cans, candy wrappers, and busted flipflops wherever they landed?

The sale went through with only the tiniest announcement buried in the back pages of the *Gazette*. The caution tape and posted signs were the first any of us heard of it.

Laughing, nervously, we ducked under the tape and made our way down to the hole where we'd swam all our lives. The cops arrived and bull-horned over the river that we were trespassing and had five minutes to vacate or risk arrest.

Men who had grown up there swimming with us turned their faces away when we reminded them of the summers we'd shared. They were just doing their jobs, they said.

The river still belonged to the town and some of us could make it down the opposite river bank, but it was a steep climb and likely to land you splayed and broken on the slate shelf that decked the river, worn smooth by spring and fall floods.

A group of us showed up at the next council meeting and took turns airing our grievances during the public comment portion until we were told our time was up. Two members of the council agreed that something should be done. Three members and the Mayor, who could regularly be found golfing with Jeff Martin during the week when the rest of us were at work, said this was a matter of private property now. They'd followed all required procedures in the sale and if we'd had a problem with it we should have spoken up then.

Three Sundays in a row we protested, crowded by the side of the road with our clever signs and a spirit of camaraderie. The *Gazette* reporter showed up. Took pictures and asked us questions, scribbling in her notebook as we answered, but we never did see a story in the paper.

Our numbers dwindled until it was just me, a handful of folks who protested everything, and the cops telling us once again it was time to move along.

No matter where I was or what I was doing, the swimming hole and Jeff Martin were there in the back of my mind throbbing like a hammer-hit thumb.

It wasn't right.

And there was nothing I could do about it.

My husband, Andy, told me I needed to let it go. We, of all people—two men whose right to love each other out in public hadn't been recognized even half our lives—should know there are bigger worries in the world than the local swimming hole. Racism, sexism, all the isms, and a climate crisis to boot. I shouldn't hold it against the folks who had lost interest, preoccupied with the business of living.

I went to the river, picked my way down the steep side as the sun set and looked for the ghosts of summers past. I imagined myself teaching the child we thought we might adopt how to swim, tossing them over my shoulders, clapping at their underwater somersaults. Giving them the things my father had given me.

Sitting there, head in my hands, I worried Andy was right—this powerless feeling would consume me if I let it and there were far worse wrongs to confront. Better to change myself than give in to the growing resentment of people who didn't care enough to take back what had been given away out from under them.

A voice startled me out of my ruminations.

"Why so down, friend?"

A three-quarters moon had risen over the placid river, lighting the snaking lines of current, wet stone bank, and the leaves of trees lining the top of the gorge on either side. I couldn't spot a soul. A splash in the river caught my attention, and there, in the middle, a salmon the size of a two-year-old swam a lazy circle and asked the question again.

Of course I'd heard of this fish. You can't walk a block in this town without meeting someone who knows someone who almost hooked it, or heard it speak, or watched it leap fifty feet in the air in acrobatic delight. Even my father believed it was as old as the town.

So here was my madness, finally emerging. Well, what can you do but answer when a fish asks a question twice?

I told it my troubles. Explained about Jeff Martin and the town council and the aching maw in my chest for all the friends and neighbors content to let another piece of what should be ours be pirated off by a handful of people.

The fish dipped under the water and I thought I had bored it, but then its head reappeared. "You're a good egg, friend," it said, "so I'm going to do you a solid. A good egg for a good egg." It laughed at its joke in a voice like a hard summer rain. It rolled over, water shimmering off its moon-silvered scales, and popped a small shining orb out of its vent. With a flick of its tail, it lobbed the egg over to me. It glowed orange in my hand, no bigger than a pea. "In three days, when the moon is full, make a wish and eat that." The salmon swam a circle and again came to a stop. "All the usual reminders about being careful what you wish for. You only get the one." And with that it swam off.

I carried the egg home, cradled in my palm, and not knowing what else to do with it, I filled a glass with water and dropped it in.

I told Andy my story and he peered at the little glob at the bottom of the glass. He put the back of his hand up to my forehead. I shrugged him off.

"I'm feeling fine."

"Okay," he said in that way that meant *if you say so*, and asked me what I was going to wish for. I shrugged again and he left me in the kitchen, watching the egg do nothing.

Over the next three days I imagined all manner of wicked ends for Jeff Martin as I worked. If not death, then public humiliations that left him impoverished. In my kinder moods, I considered wishing him a change of heart. A Scroogening. But wasn't there always another Jeff Martin, waiting to take his place?

I thought of personal gain—a windfall of money that would set Andy and I up for life. But then I would be the Jeff Martin, wouldn't I?

On the third night, when the moon rose full and gleaming, I stood on our front lawn and wished the wish of my heart: that good people believed they could make a difference if they tried. I drank the glass of water, the glowing egg sliding over my tongue and down my throat.

I slipped into bed and apologized to Andy for not wishing something for us.

He laughed, "don't be a fool," and kissed me until we were peeling each other's sweats off in the dark.

In the morning, I walked down to the diner for a cup of coffee before work, hoping to find the world changed.

But it was just as it had been the morning before. The *Gazette* followed a developer looking to tear down waterfront buildings and put up luxury condos along the lake. Old white men grumbled at the counter about immigrants taking away jobs, and when I got to work the foreman told our crew we'd have to put in extra hours to make sure the plumbing was roughed in on schedule, but we'd be shorted hours next week so the company didn't have to pay overtime.

Frustrated and exhausted, I got home no longer furious only with Jeff Martin and the people who wouldn't stand up to him, but with myself, for having hoped. Color drained out of the world. Everywhere I looked were signs of the inevitability of everything crumbling to shit.

Andy tried to cheer me, but most evenings ended with me scrolling through the news, finding proof of all the terrible things in the world and the myriad ways people make each other suffer. I had been earnest and optimistic and what had it gotten me? Nothing but a broken heart.

My neighbors were right. Better to tend to your own affairs and hope the burning world arrived at your doorstep last.

Three weeks into my festering, I arrived home to find Andy sitting at the kitchen table, a stack of papers in front of him. I eyed them as I bent to kiss him and he nodded for me to sit down. He handed a page over to me, a yellow stick-on arrow pointing to a signature line, "Sign there."

"Wha—"

"Just sign."

He was trying to play it serious, like he was in the law office where he worked as a paralegal and I was some client in a suit and tie.

But you don't spend fifteen years with a person and not know when they're buzzing to tell you something, so I played along.

I signed three different papers before he hit me with the sidelong smile—his charming snaggletooth crooked and jaunty—that first caught my attention all those years ago. He unfolded a surveyor's map, smoothed it across the table. There was Jeff Martin's house, devil horns drawn out of the roof and a fish penciled in the swimming hole. I followed Andy's finger down to a spot marked with an X.

"About seventy feet south of the swimming hole, the Jenkin's property line starts." He pointed to a spot where the river swung a wide arc away from Valley Road and back towards Banks Road before tumbling down a series of small waterfalls out into the inlet and beyond that, the lake. "Liza has agreed to deed access rights for this portion of land," he circled a rectangle formed by dotted lines, "to the Friends of the River. A nonprofit of which you and I are the founding members. It's steep, but you can build a good set of stairs that would do the trick and then it's just a matter of walking up the bank," his finger trailed back up to the swimming hole.

The world was still on fire, the wealthy were still fucking over as many people as they could, and all manner of horrible shit still needed to be torn down. But look at this man and how he loved me.

I started on the stairs that weekend, clearing a path through the brush and saplings from the street to the cliff edge. About an hour into my work Liza Jenkin's daughter, home from college, arrived with a tool belt slung over her shoulder and a cooler of cold drinks. By lunch, three more neighbors had come to lend a hand.

We worked every Saturday for a month, our numbers growing so large that half of us were just standing around offering encouragement and memories of summers past (somebody's story of a talking fish got us all sharing our own).

Where one person's knowledge faltered—the sturdiest way to anchor the stairs to the rock face, where to get the best price on this material or that—another stood up and offered what they could.

When it was finished we made our way up to the swimming hole, laughing and whooping, our voices amplified off the gorge walls. We cannonballed, or waded in, or sat on the rock-shelf and dangled our toes, and no matter how many police cars Martin called they couldn't stop our jubilee.

E. C. Barrett (she/they) writes folk horror, fabulism and dark speculative fiction. She is or has been an academic, journalist, bookseller, editor, and obituary writer. A Clarion West graduate, E. C. has stories in *Bourbon Penn*, *Baffling Magazine* and elsewhere. E. C. is queer, neurodivergent, and enjoys more maker hobbies than is entirely practical. ecbarrett.com

How to Get Away with Chaining Myself to my Friends in Front of Heavy Duty Machinery

Abbie Goldberg

"If we ever wanted to, our friend group could transition nicely into a BDSM circle," I announce to my friend George as we stare at nearly $1,000 worth of locks and chains in a pile on the living room floor.

"Is that a thing? A BDSM circle?" he asks, looking up from his project of color-coding keys to locks with iridescent nail polish.

"I don't know." I shrug. "You can ask the cops about it."

"Probably not the best strategy. . . ." he says as he sets up a stopwatch.

"Ok! Let's try Pancakes with Blueberries." The code name for the position we've chosen doesn't sound like the sexiest of moves, but we haven't chosen it to be sexy. After all, we are not (as of now) a BDSM circle. We are just friends, with a lot of locks, a lot of chains, and a plan to shut down a natural gas pipeline.

I got involved in activism my senior year of high school. For my first act of civil disobedience, I skipped school to attend a rally in Washington, DC against the Keystone XL pipeline. High school tyrant Mr. Maxfield told me that if I went, he'd give me detention. As an anxious teen whose identity hinged on straight As and approving nods from adults, I cried about the decision beforehand to no less than three teachers and two administrators. But the next Saturday, wearing my homemade No Tar Sands shirt in the no phone zone cafeteria with all the other adolescent miscreants, I felt like a complete badass. Four years and many protests later, here I am searching under the couch for missing adult diapers as I prepare for my second arrest for direct action.

Today, there are six of us planning to block construction of the West Roxbury pipeline with our bodies. Ian, Amy, and I will jump in a pit where the pipeline will go and lock ourselves in a triangle with our backs together. This arrangement is 'Pancakes with Blueberries'. In a pit across town Max, Sam, and Angus will fold themselves into a complicated tangle of arms and legs, with people lying down and sitting on top of each other. This we call, somewhat less whimsically, Shit Pit Yoga.

George is driving the getaway car. We have planned to do one loop around the block to scope. The second drive-by is the real deal.

"Oh my G-d I can't do it!" Amy panics.

"No no! We're doing it!" I cheer and lunge for the door, "Oh shit. Can we do another loop?"

"Come on," says Ian, hopping out. Nothing fazes Ian.

Once we're out of the car, we must act fast. The workers and security on site are used to activists. If we don't get into formation, they'll get us out much more quickly, meaning the whole thing will have been a big waste of time and money.

The July sun is already hot at eight in the morning. I look over the edge of the pit, then close my eyes and jump, like it's a swimming pool, like it's a normal summer day and I have nothing to worry about. Like I am young and fearless.

I lock my feet together first so that even if we don't get our waists locked together I will not be able to walk away if the police try to make me. More specifically, if the police try to make me, my ankles will break. This fact that previously seemed merely strategic is suddenly anxiety-inducing. The chains have been custom tailored for my ankles by an engineering major friend. They are tight, requiring the lock to be just so to close. I close it.

For our waists, each person is in charge of the lock to their left. (Always go left.) I reach around and my clammy fingers fumble with the bolt between Ian and me. Shit. How much time has passed? 20 seconds? A month? I scoot backward to get a better angle and the lock slams shut.

"I've got pancakes!" I call out.

I wipe my hands on my pants, which are long despite the 90 degree weather because I've been told that jail is cold. I'm fighting global warming, but I still hate the cold. I wipe my hands so I'll be ready for what's next: super glue.

"It never really works," George told us weeks before in a prep meeting. "Your hands will be too sweaty from heat and nerves, but it confuses the cops and looks good in a headline."

I spread it across my palm and up my arm then pass the bottle off to Ian before we grasp hands. He passes it to Amy, and Amy throws it aside hoping we don't accrue an additional littering charge for this detritus. All hands together and no one has even noticed the commotion. We've got blueberries.

Climate change is bad. Really bad. Most of the time, even I am a climate denier. I will lay my body down in the sand, but I don't know how to grapple with the voice in my head, with the numbers in the news, with the knowledge that my country has condemned hundreds of thousands to death. People will lose their homes. People will lose their livelihoods. People will die. It's started already. And the people who will bear this burden first and hardest are communities of color, low-income, and indigenous communities. I don't know how to feel this, I mean really feel this, and still wake up in the morning. I get the urge to ignore. I get the desire to look away. Of course I deny.

In the pit, we clutch each other's hands as if they aren't already glued together.

"I'm nervous," Amy tells me. We do the only reasonable thing there is to do; we sing.

"The tide is rising, and so are we." The song comes from Rabbi Shoshana Freedman and singing it I have never felt more powerful. Shouting and sirens begin to drown our voices. We sing louder. The construction workers, police, and firemen circle us, looking down over the sandy drop off. They grumble about how to cleanse what is, for this morning, a money-losing pit of filthy activists.

Over the radio, we hear: "Wait, they're in your pit too!?"

Oh yeah we are! We are everywhere.

The fireman throws his jacket over my head to protect my eyes from flying sparks. It's heavy and I have a vague memory of elementary school field trips from back when I had a simpler understanding of what it meant to be a civil servant. Without warning, I am sprayed with a hose. This is also, in theory, to protect me, but sitting in a puddle of mud in darkness beneath a fireman's jacket, warm metal against my bruised ankles, all I can think is, *How did I get here?* Why do my friends, my beautiful friends who are in their early twenties, who navigate depression, and grad school, and dinner, and dating, why must they put themselves in situations like this? What a totally absurd thing to do with a Monday morning.

The moment I am free from my ankle chains, I am bound at the wrists.

"You're under arrest for trespassing and disturbing the peace."

Personally, I thought our music was perfectly peaceful, but the National Lawyers Guild, who provides legal aid to activists, says arguments based on the quality of the singing will not hold up in a court of law.

As I am led past two fire trucks and an ambulance to the police wagon, I call out to my jail support an important message, "Please bring pizza!"

In the first holding cell, we cheer as Max, Angus, and Sam are led in.

"We love you!" Max, whose baby will be born within the week, has a towel wrapped around his waist.

"What happened to your pants??" we ask.

"Well . . . ." Max monotones, "Sam was screaming because of the superglue and they poured acetone on my dick."

"What??"

But Max is led to the back to be fingerprinted.

"I guess it's good he's already having his baby." Ian shrugs. Nothing fazes Ian.

Here is the truth. The sacrifices we will have to make are going to be bigger than $40 and a day in jail. Change is happening, but not fast enough. At this point we are not fighting to stop climate change. Our fight is for degrees. Degrees of warming. Degrees of deaths.

To those who would call young activists idealistic I would say, yeah. The criminal justice system is racist, and cruel, and life-ruining. But because I am white, young, college-educated, and protesting climate change in a liberal-leaning region, I am free to pass through its tendrils relatively unscathed. And I would be lying to say it's not partially for selfish reasons that I engage in civil disobedience. I am terrified by the thought that the fires, storms, droughts, and hostility to immigrants and refugees we see now may not in fact be "the new normal". The new normal will, in all likelihood, be a lot worse.

There's kind of a relief in jail that at this moment, there's nothing more I can do. In my cell, with nothing but my tired mind, receding adrenaline, and wet clothes, I can finally accept that this is out of my control. It is unacceptable to live resigned to the reality that we will not be able to do enough. It's self-sustaining to acknowledge this truth. People will lose their homes, communities, and livelihoods. People will die. Hopefully fewer because of us, but there's really no way to know. We will keep fighting anyway. We will sing louder. We sing to be heard, but also to say, "We hear you. We have not, and we will not, forget you."

The marches and rallies, the meetings and pits have all taught me how to love. This is the way I have to say "I have your back" to Amy and Ian and George and Sam and Max, to our unborn (or soon to be born) children, to my sisters, to the fighters everywhere. There is no winning in a world where people will die needlessly, but there is still loving. There is still believing in a world worth fighting for. When we are singing, when we are laughing, this is when I find the strength, trust, and commitment to lay my body down.

Outside the jail, my hands oily with pizza grease, I hug my friends as they're released. On Sunday, we'll debrief the action in our normal meeting and eat home-cooked chili from a comically large pot. We will think about how we can confuse the police for longer, how we can maintain pressure, how we can engage more people in West Roxbury. We'll break out the ukulele and play John Prine crooners. For now, I run and jump on Angus as he walks from the precinct.

"Angus!!!!! We did it!" I cheer.

"Oh my G-d did you actually get us pizza? I'm so happy!" he says to George, who is without a doubt the best jail support a grimy activist could ask for.

"Of course!" George smiles. He yells to the precinct as we walk to the car, "See you next week!"

Next week, there will be a new pit to fill with new songs. Next week, we will be everywhere.

Abbie Goldberg is a multidisciplinary artist from the mountains of rural Maine. They are an alumnus of Broadway Advocacy Coalition's Theater of Change program, The New Opera and Musical Theater Initiative, the Join for Justice Community Organizing Fellowship, and New York University's Graduate Musical Theatre Writing program. Their work has been performed at Lincoln Center, Joe's Pub, Rattlestick Theater, Salt Tree Eco Puppetry Festival, Rockwood Music Hall, and more. Their writing has been published by *HowlRound*, *Autostraddle*, *Dame*, *Waif*, *The Theatre Times*, *Sinister Wisdom*, *AK Press*, *Ben Yehuda Press* and more. They are passionate about using joy and spectacle as forces for social change.

Bonus Content

C. G. Aubrey

Neurodivergent, adjective [English] (neu·ro·di·ver·gent)
: having or relating to a disorder or condition (such as autism spectrum disorder, attention deficit hyperactivity disorder, dyslexia, or obsessive-compulsive disorder) that impacts the way the brain processes information : exhibiting or characteristic of variations in typical neurological development.[1]

Neurodiversity, noun [English] (neu·ro·di·ver·si·ty)
1: individual differences in brain functioning regarded as normal variations within the human population
2: the concept that differences in brain functioning within the human population are normal, that brain functioning that is not neurotypical should not be stigmatized, and that people with neurodivergent brain functioning should not be excluded from groups, organizations, etc.[2]

"[The neurodiversity paradigm] challenges us to reexamine all categories and concepts that currently fall under the pathology paradigm, lest it turn out we have wrongly medicalized suffering in any strand of human life that might better be accounted for in terms of social marginalization and oppression."[3]

Important Notes

The words "neurodivergent" and "neurodiversity" are rooted in the English language and English speaking and cultural contexts.

Definitions of neurodivergence and disabilities (as with other marginalizations) are culturally and societally ascribed. What is labeled

1. Merriam-Webster.com Dictionary, s.v. "neurodivergent," accessed September 12, 2025, https://www.merriam-webster.com/dictionary/neurodivergent.
2. Merriam-Webster.com Dictionary, s.v. "neurodiversity," accessed September 12, 2025, https://www.merriam-webster.com/dictionary/neurodiversity.
3. Robert Chapman. "Neurodiversity Theory and Its Discontents: Autism, Schizophrenia, and the Social Model of Disability," The Bloomsbury Companion to Philosophy of Psychiatry, Bloomsbury Publishing, 2019 (pp. 371-390).

as such in one culture may not be in another.

While we will often find "neurodivergent" and "neurodiversity" used together, it is important to understand that "neurodiversity" and the Neurodiversity Movement represent a paradigm shift from pathology to diversity. This shift, however, does not (and should not) include the very real and disabling experiences of neurodivergent individuals.

Further Reading on Neurodiversity

- "Neurodiversity: a Brief History," Neurodiversity@ Caltech. https://neurodiversity.caltech.edu/resources/neurodiversity-a-brief-history
- Baaumer, Nicole, MD, MEd and Julia Frueh, MD. "What is Neurodiversity?" *Harvard Health Publishing*, November 23, 2021. https://www.health.harvard.edu/blog/what-is-neurodiversity-202111232645
- Chapman, Robert. *Empire of Normality: Neurodiversity and Capitalism*, Pluto Press, 2023.
- Nair, V. K., Farah, W., & Boveda, M. (2024). "Is neurodiversity a Global Northern White paradigm?, *Autism*, 0(0). https://doi.org/10.1177/13623613241280835
- Omeiza KA (2024). *Autistic and Black: Our Experiences of Growth, Progress, and Empowerment*. London: Jessica Kingsley Publishers. ISBN 9781839976209.
- Praslova LN. "Autism Doesn't Hold People Back at Work. Discrimination Does". *Harvard Business Review*, December 13, 2021
- Tougaw, Jason. "Neurodiversity: the Movement," *Psychology Today* (O), April 18, 2020. https://www.psychologytoday.com/us/blog/the-elusive-brain/202004/neurodiversity-the-movement
- Österborg, Sofia. "The Neurodiversity Movement and the Nordic Countries," *nordics.info*, Aarhus University, February 7, 2025. https://nordics.info/nnl/show/artikel/introduction-to-the-neurodiversity-movement-in-the-nordic-countries

A Sampling of Organizations Related to Specific Neurodivergences[4]

- Attention Deficit Disorder Association (ADDA) https://add.org/
- Autism Self Advocacy Network https://autisticadvocacy.org/
- Anxiety and Depression Association of America https://adaa.org/
- Black Neurodiversity https://www.blackneurodivevrsity.com/
- International Dyslexia Association https://dyslexiaida.org/
- ION-Institute of Neurodiversity https://ioneurodiversity.org/
- Kaleidoscope Society https://www.kaleidoscopesociety.com/
- Therapist Neurodiversity Collective [International] https://therapistndc.org/
- TS Around the World https://www.tourettes-action.org.uk/75-ts-around-the-world.html
- World Autism Organization https://worldautismorganisation.com/ [accessible in over one hundred languages]

More Cool Stuff

- Aldrige, James. "What's Neurodivergence Got to Do With It?", Climate Museum UK, February 01, 2025. https://climatemuseumuk.org/2025/02/01/whats neurodivergence-got-to-do-with-it/
- Martin, Chris. "The Listening World: Neurodivergent Poets from Unrestricted Interest," the Poetry Society of America. https://poetrysociety.org/poems-essays/on-poetry/on-the-listenting-world
- *Unrestricted Interest.* An Organization co-founded by Chris Martin that is "an organization dedicated to helping neurodivergent learners transform their lives through writing." www.unrestrictedinterest.com
- "Unrestricted Interest," New York Public Library Exhibit. https://www.nypl.org/events/exhibitions/community-showcases/unrestricted-interest

4. This sampling should in no way read as an endorsement from us, simply a starting place for personal education.

- Martinez, Chloe. "Neurodivergent People Find Solace in Wild Places (and the planet benefits from it)," Sierra, April 2025. https://www.sierra-club.org/sierra/2025-1-spring/critic-s-notebook/neurodivergent-people-find-solace-wild-places
- McNamara, B. "The Kaleidoscope Society Is Smashing ADHD Stigma for Women and Girls". *Teen Vogue*, December 12, 2016. https://www.teenvogue.com/story/kaleidoscope-society-adhd-stigma-women-girls
- Redhead, Eve. "How neurodiversity can impact climate action," *bulletin**, The University of Edinburgh, (April 24, 2024). https://bulletin.ed.ac.uk/2024/04/24/how-neurodiversity-can-impact-climate-action/

www.ingramcontent.com/pod-product-compliance
Lightning Source LLC
Chambersburg PA
CBHW021730190726
48288CB00009B/2989

* 9 7 8 1 9 5 5 3 6 0 1 6 6 *